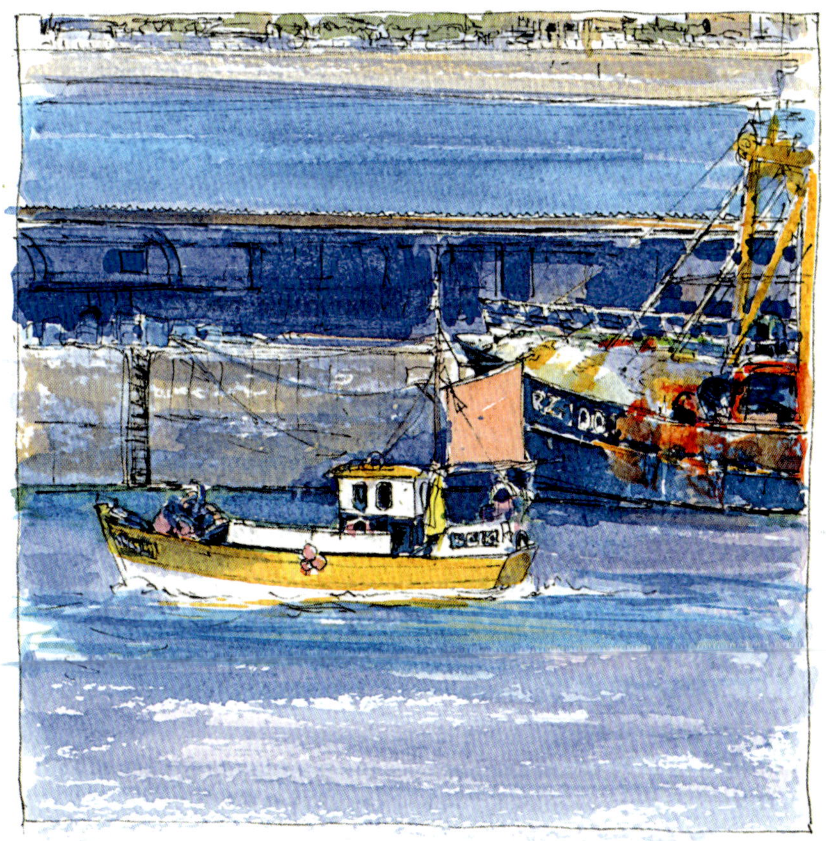

Sue Lewington

NEWLYN

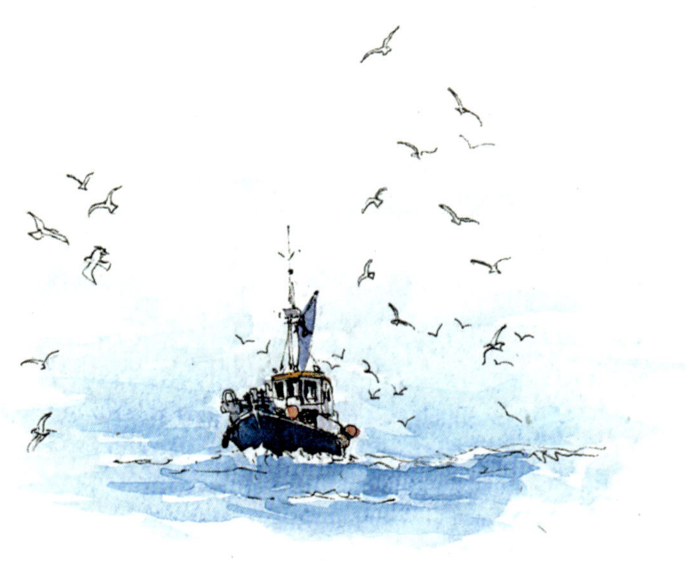

Published by Truran
Truran is an imprint of Tor Mark, United Downs Industrial Estate,
St. Day, Redruth, Cornwall   TR16 5HY
First published in 2016. This reprint 2021
ISBN 978 1 85022 250 7

Printed and bound the UK

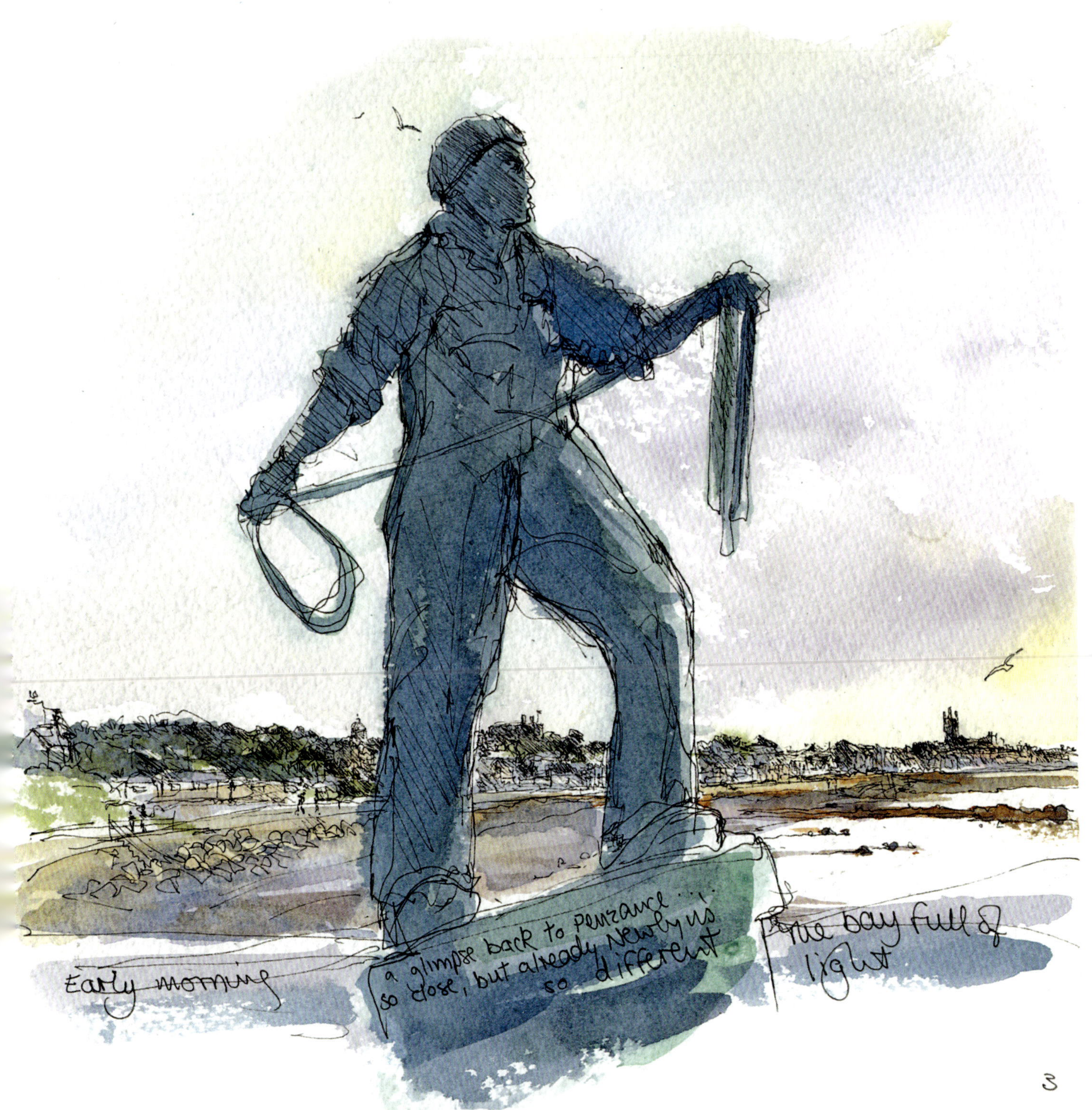
Early morning
a glimpse back to Penzance...
so close, but already Newlyn is
so different
the bay full of light

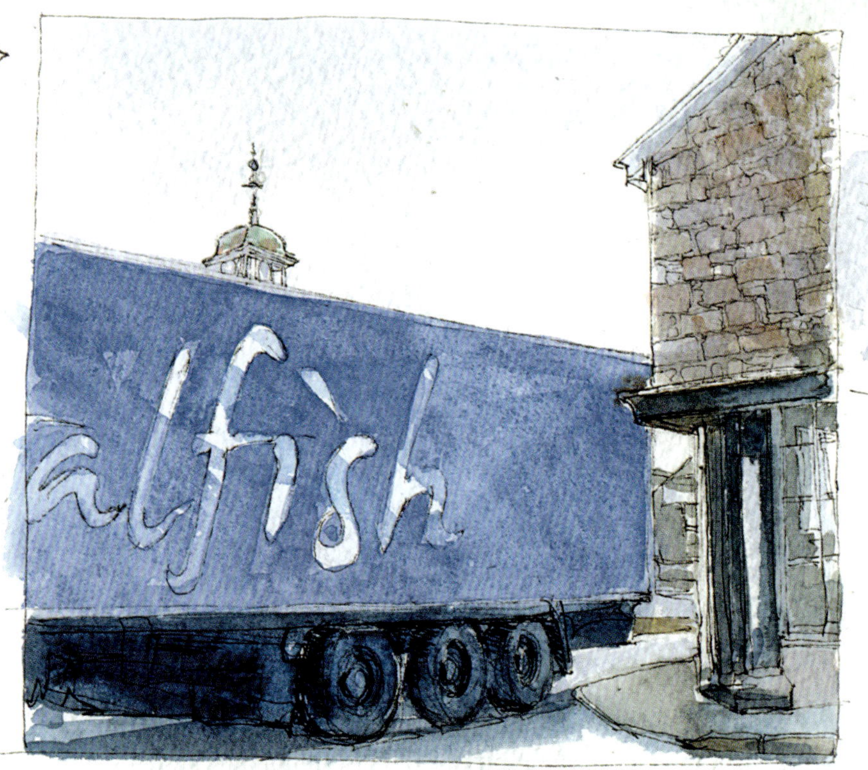

The first rule of drawing outside —
If it can move it will move.
second rule —
If it can't move something will
park between you & it . . . .

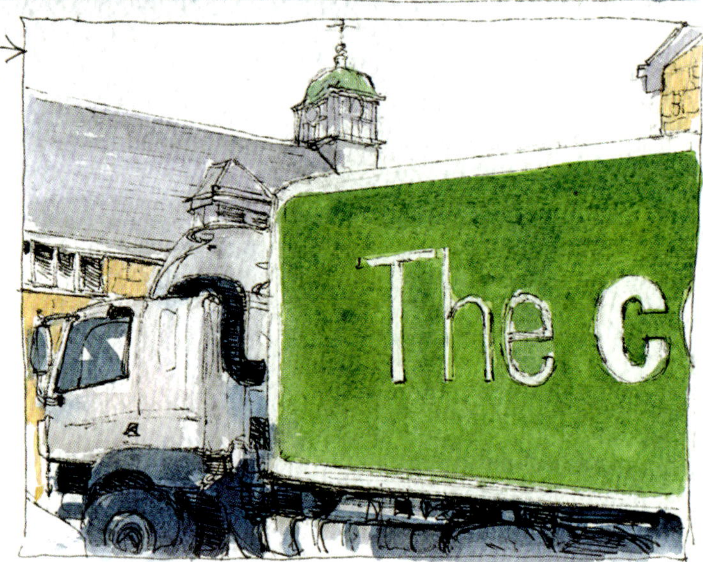

4

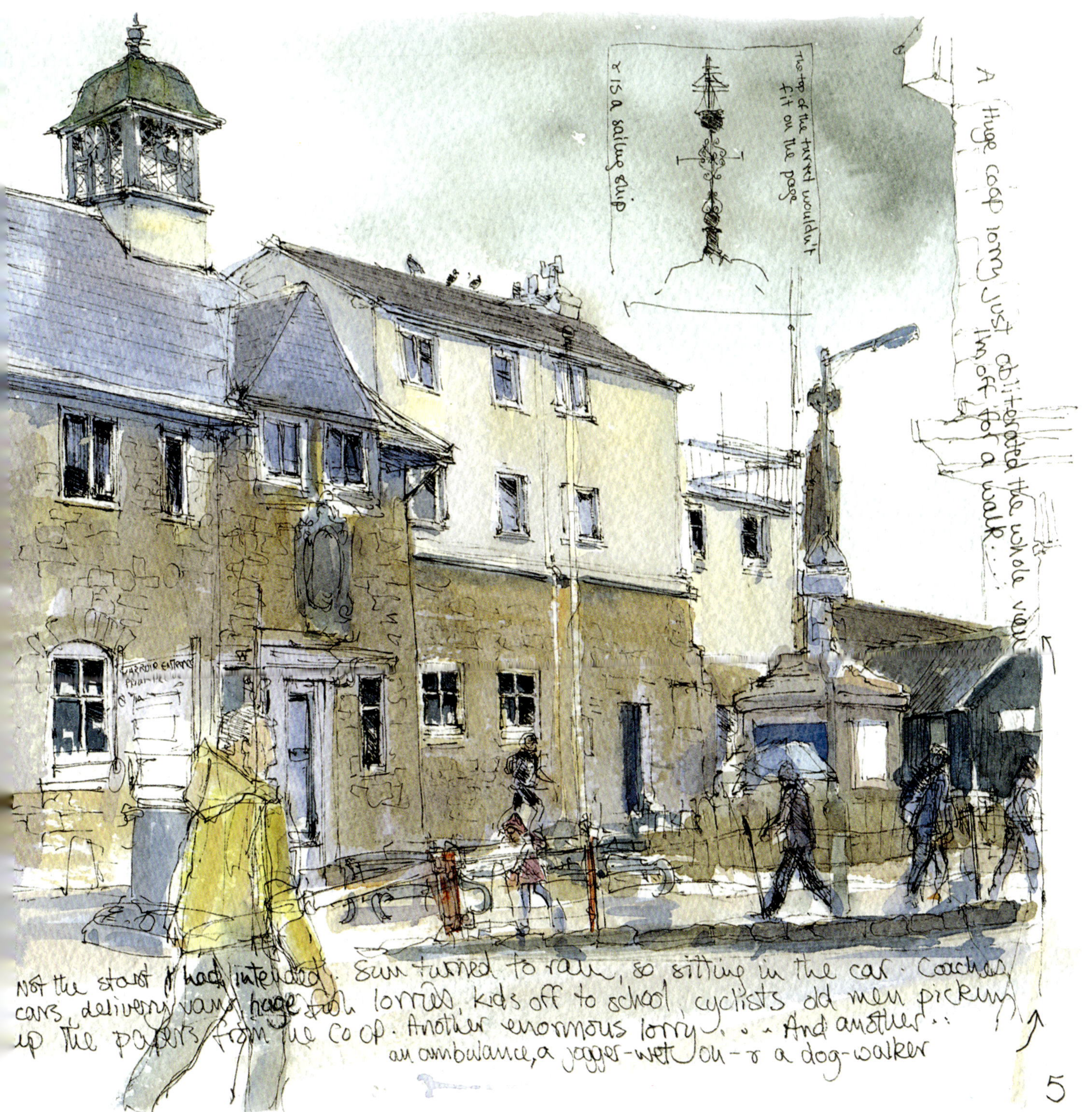

r IS a sailing ship.
The top of the turret wouldn't fit on the page
A huge coop lorry just obliterated the whole view — I'm off for a walk...
Not the start I had intended. Sun turned to rain, so sitting in the car. Coaches, cars, delivery vans, huge fish lorries, kids off to school, cyclists, old men picking up the papers from the co op. Another enormous lorry... — And another... an ambulance, a jogger-wet! oh — r a dog-walker

5

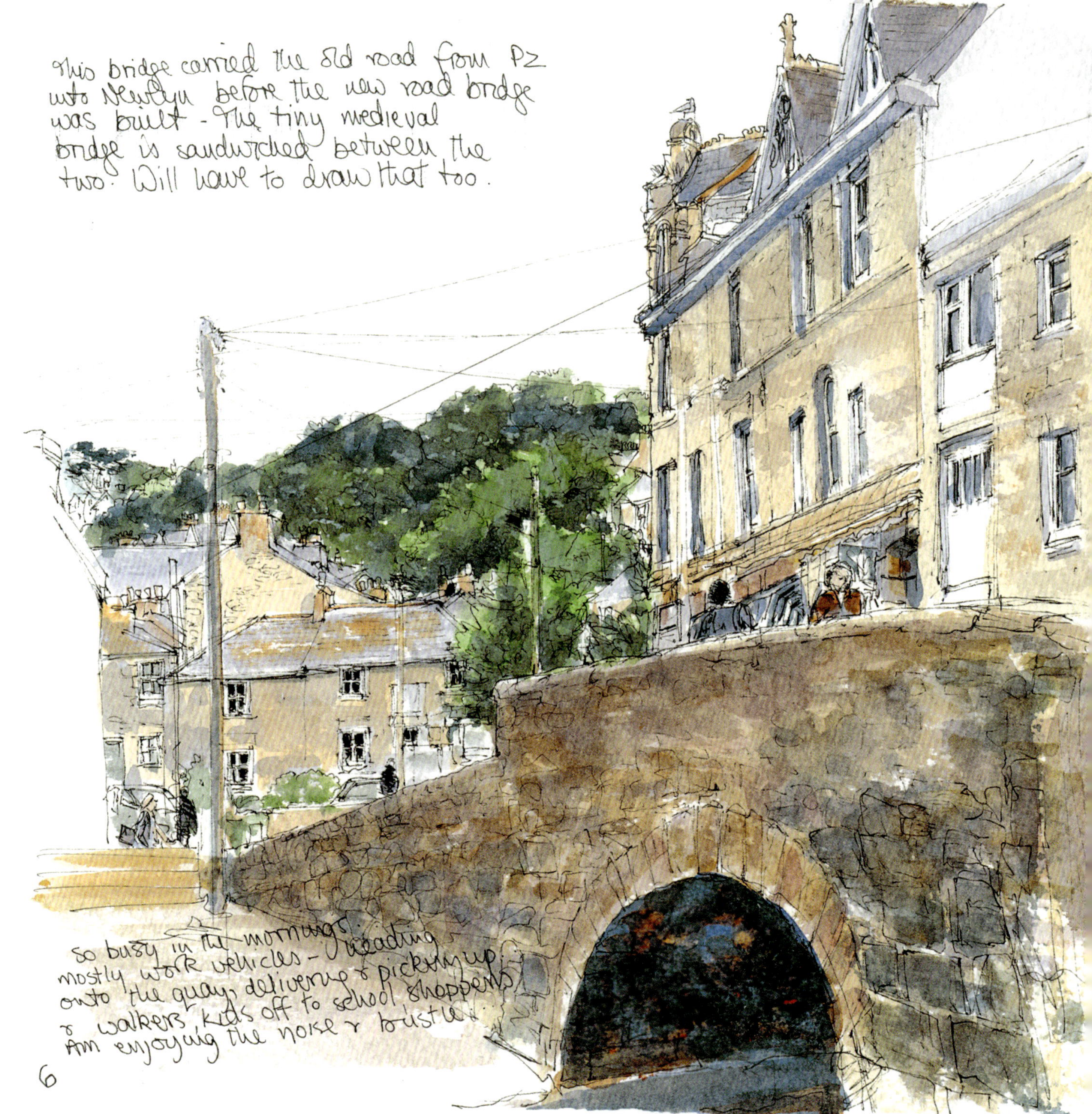
This bridge carried the old road from PZ
into Newlyn before the new road bridge
was built - The tiny medieval
bridge is sandwiched between the
two. Will have to draw that too.
So busy in the mornings. Heading
mostly work vehicles - heading
onto the quay, delivering & picking up.
& walkers, kids off to school shoppers.
Am enjoying the noise & bustle.
6

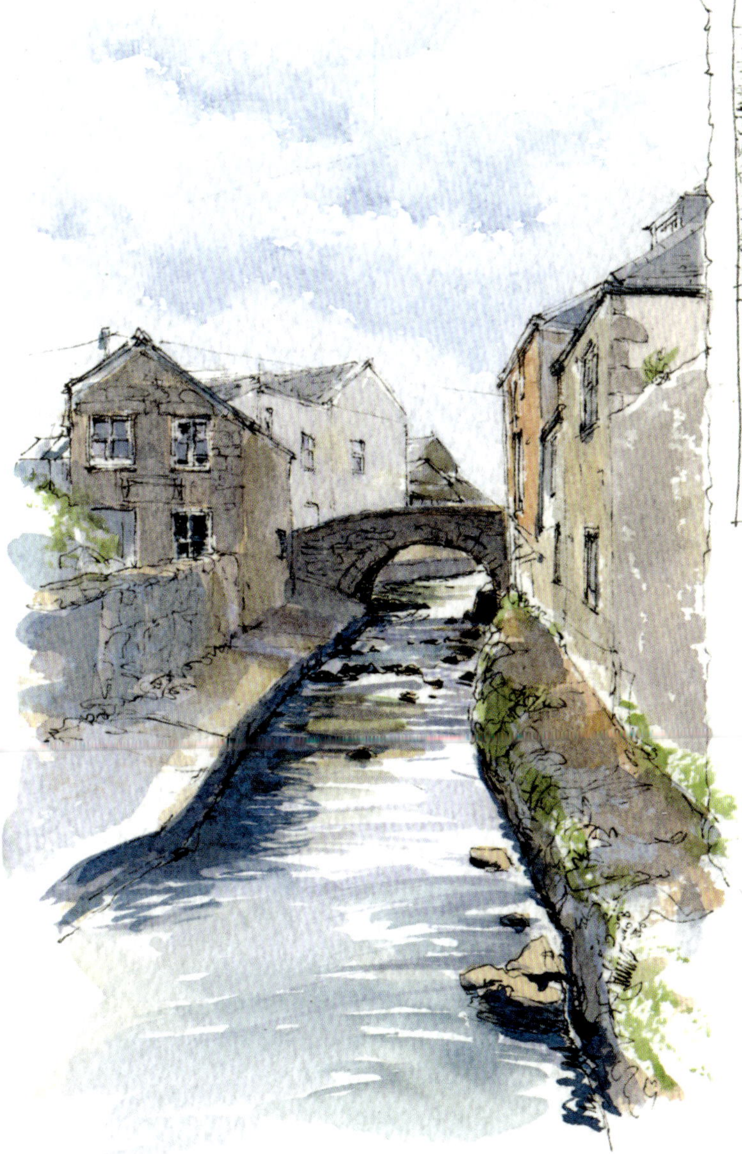

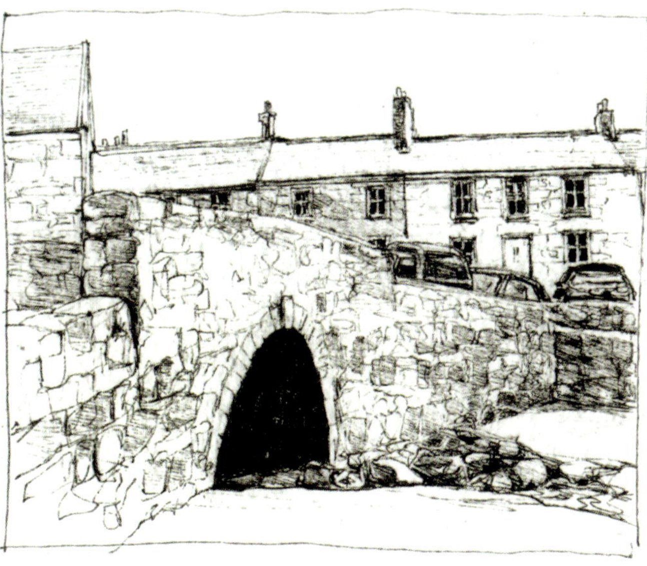

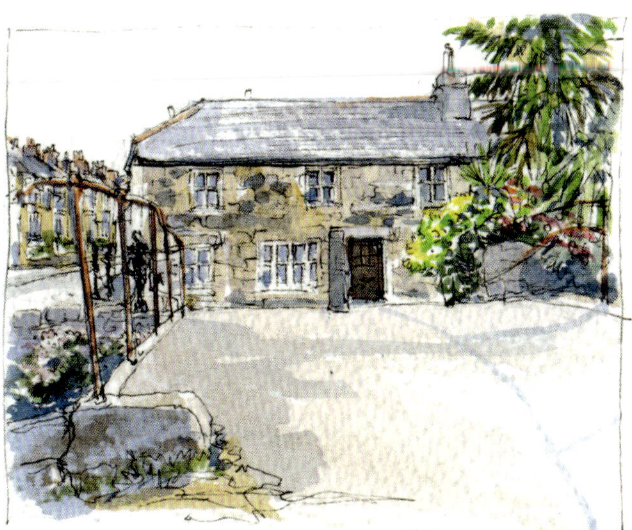

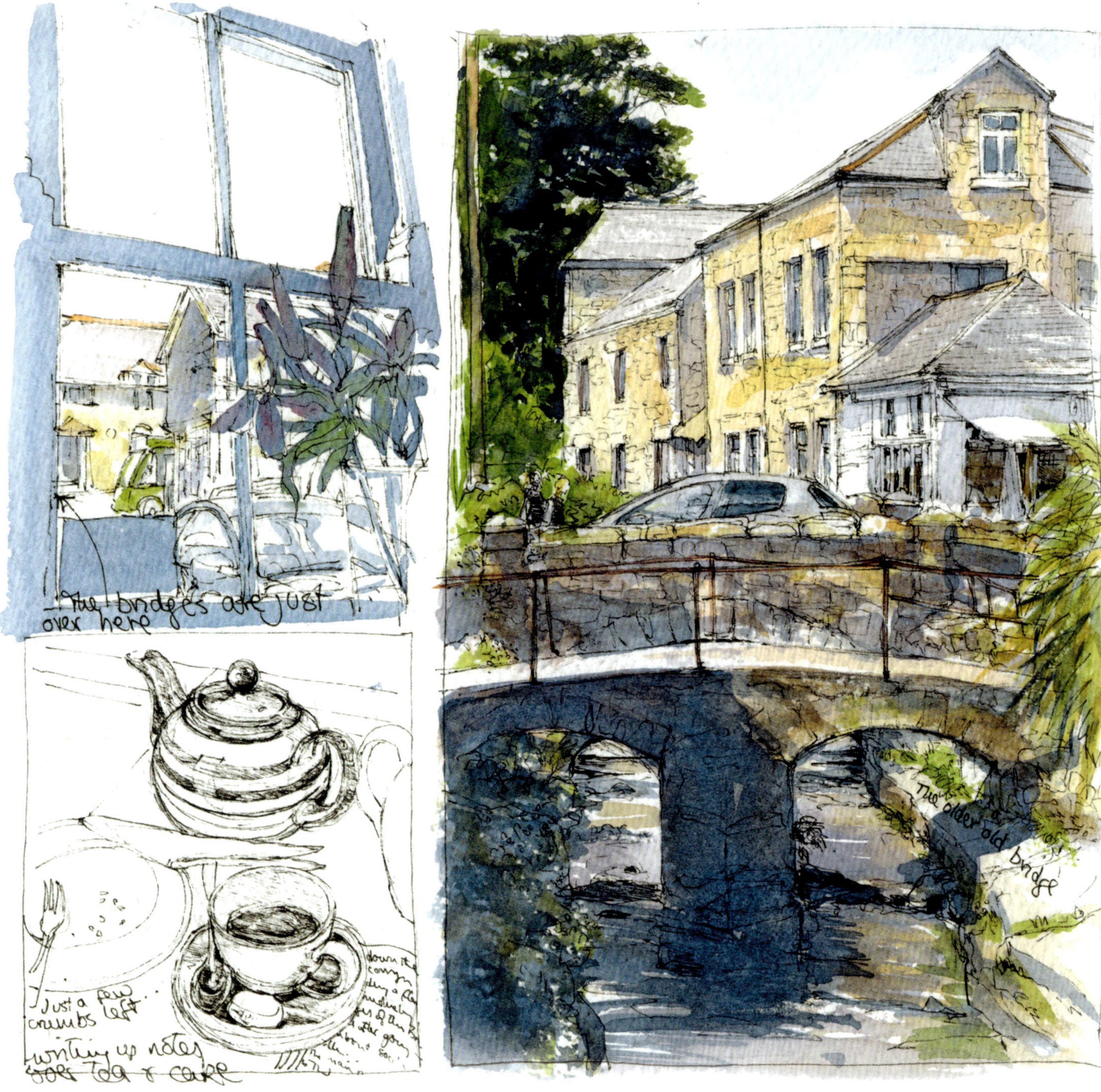

The bridges are just over here
The older old bridge
Just a few crumbs left
writing up notes goes tea & cake

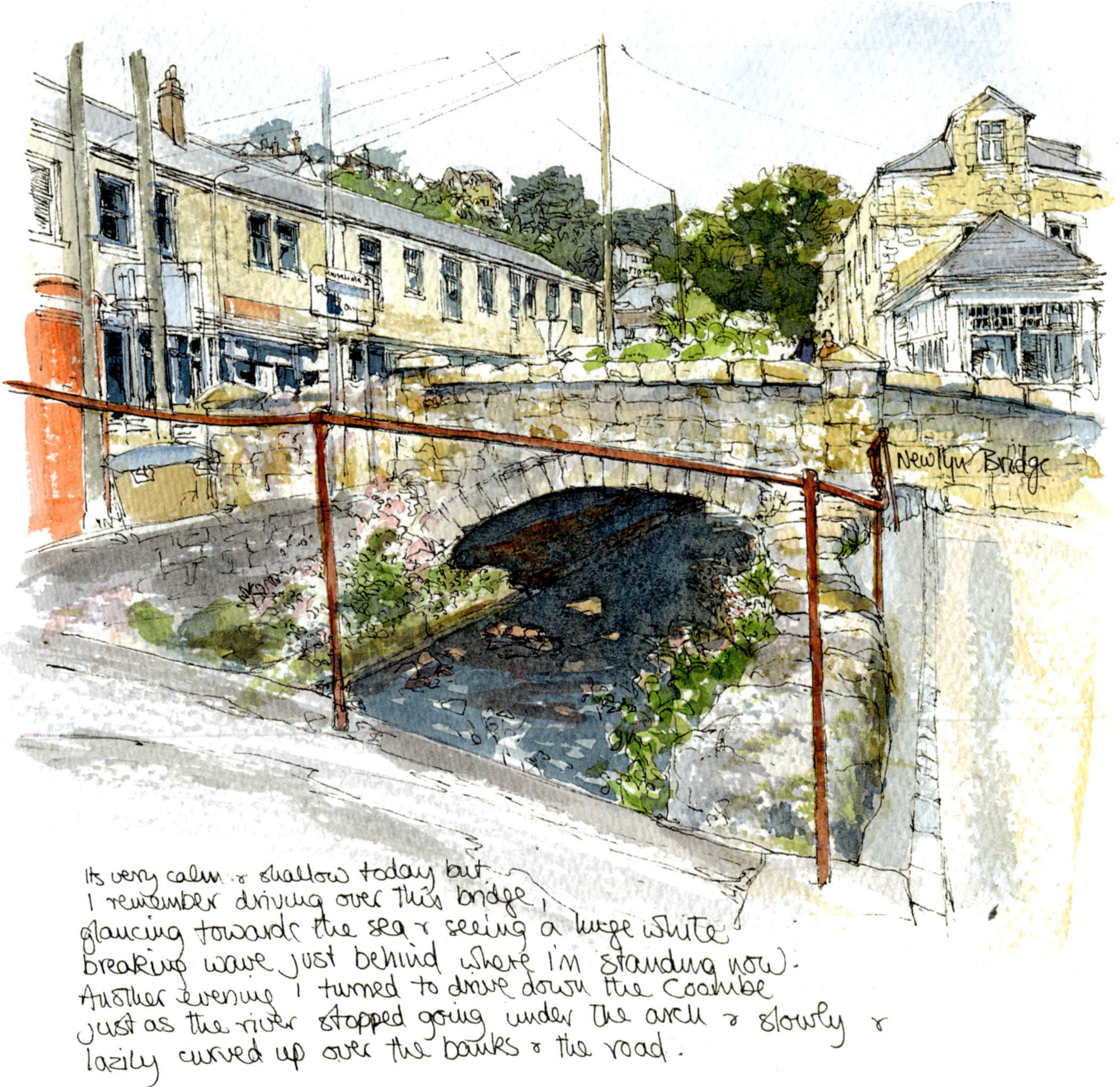

Its very calm & shallow today but
I remember driving over this bridge,
glancing towards the sea & seeing a huge white
breaking wave just behind where I'm standing now.
Another evening I turned to drive down the Coombe
just as the river stopped going under the arch & slowly &
lazily curved up over the banks & the road.

9

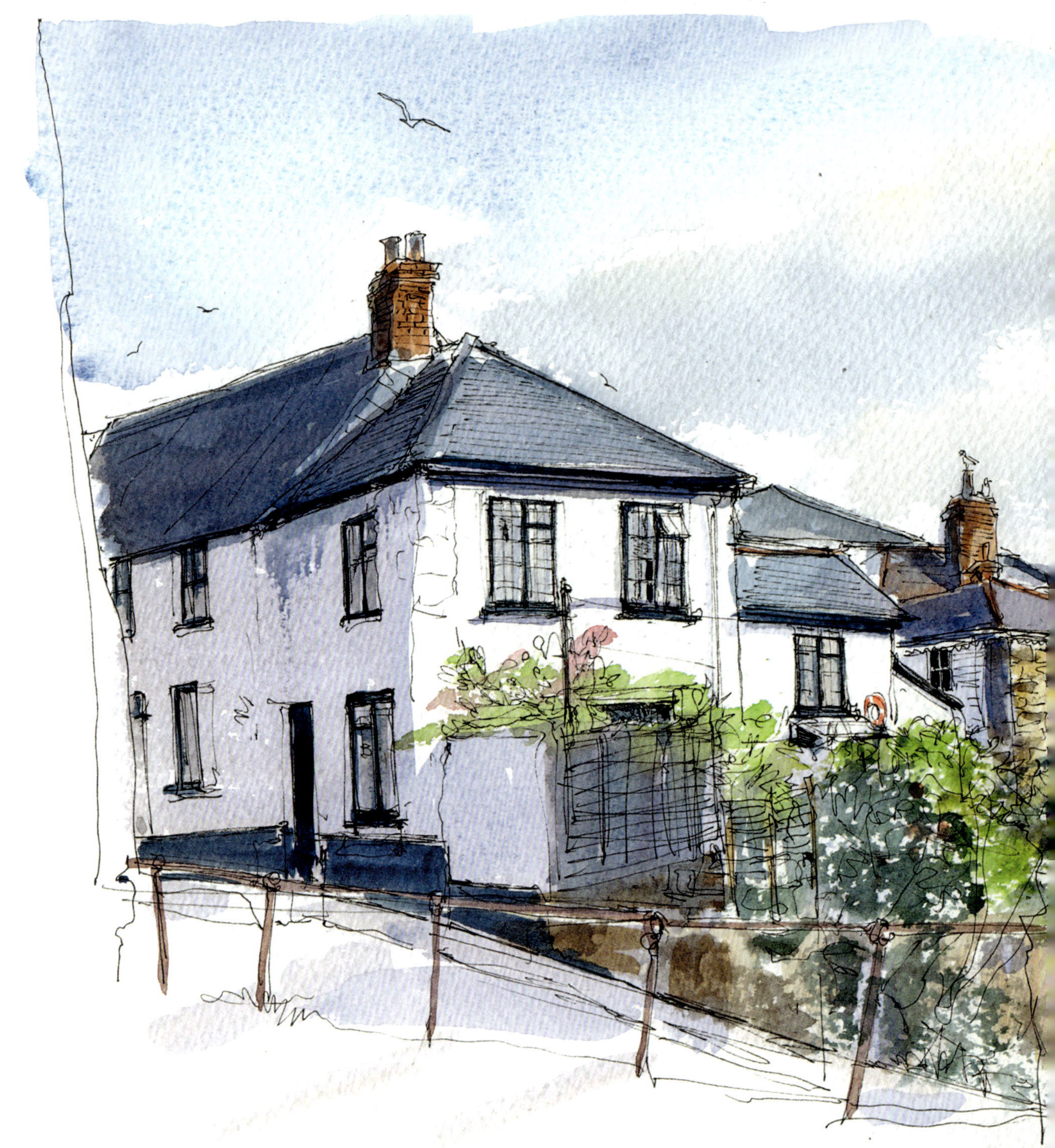

10

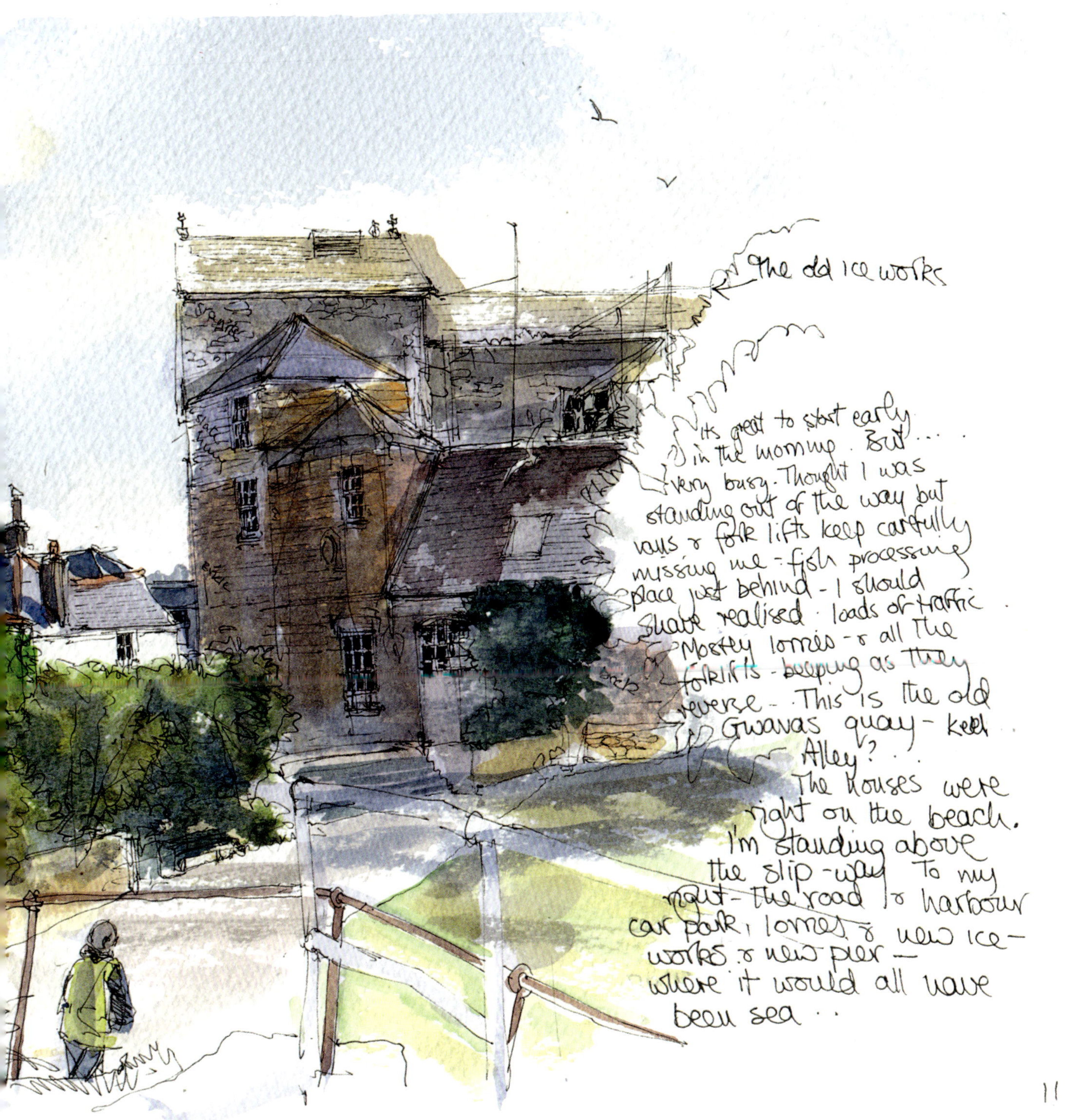
The old ice works

Its great to start early
in the morning. But...
very busy. Thought I was
standing out of the way but
vans & fork lifts keep carfully
missing me - fish processing
place just behind - I should
have realised. loads of traffic
- Mostly lorries - & all the
forklifts - beeping as they
reverse - This is the old
Gwavas quay - keel
Alley?
The houses were
right on the beach.
I'm standing above
the slip-way. To my
right - the road & harbour
car park, lorries & new ice-
works & new pier —
where it would all have
been sea ..

11

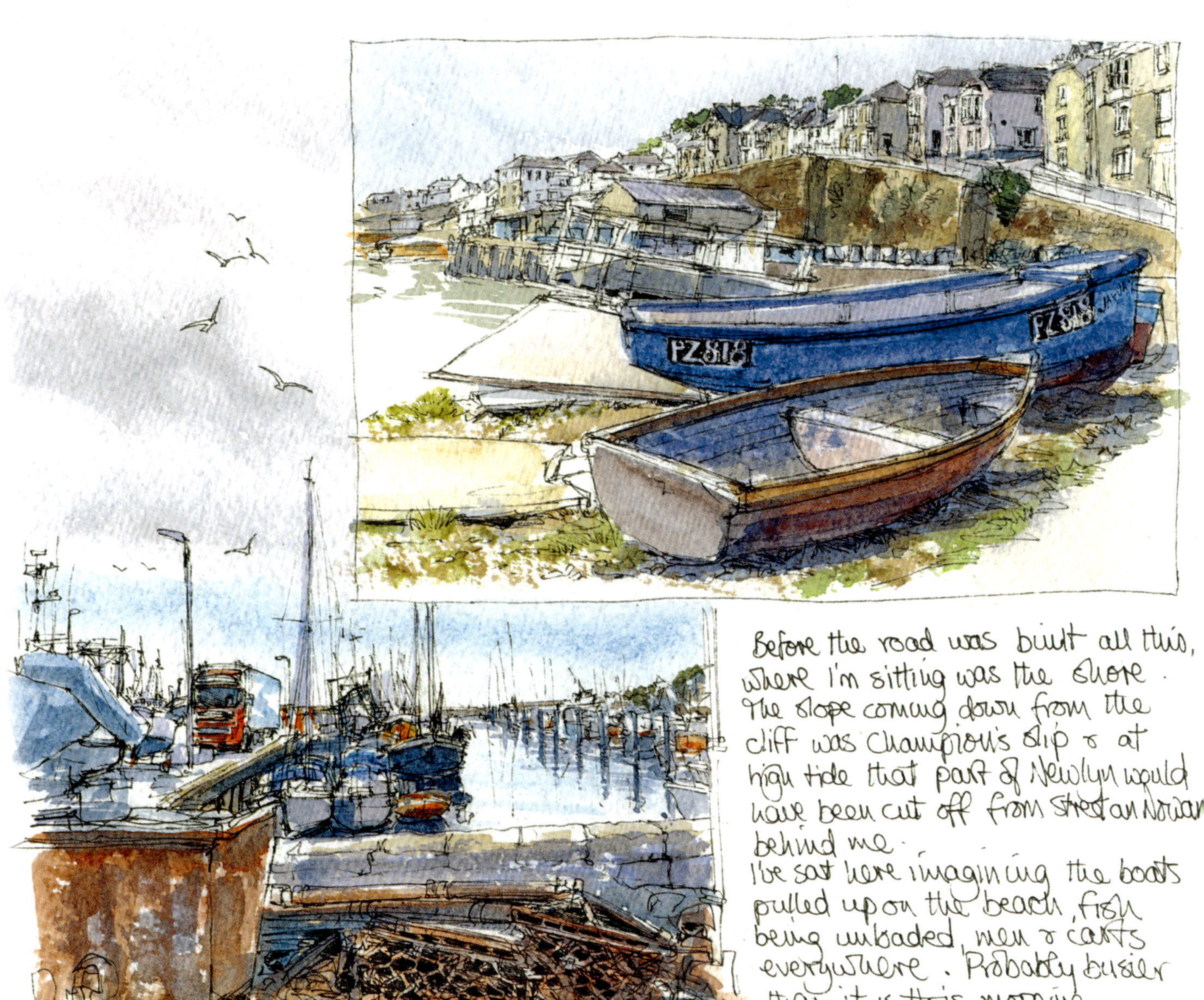

Before the road was built all this,
where I'm sitting was the shore.
The slope coming down from the
cliff was Champion's slip & at
high tide that part of Newlyn would
have been cut off from Street an Nowan
behind me.
I've sat here imagining the boats
pulled up on the beach, fish
being unloaded, men & carts
everywhere. Probably busier
than it is this morning.

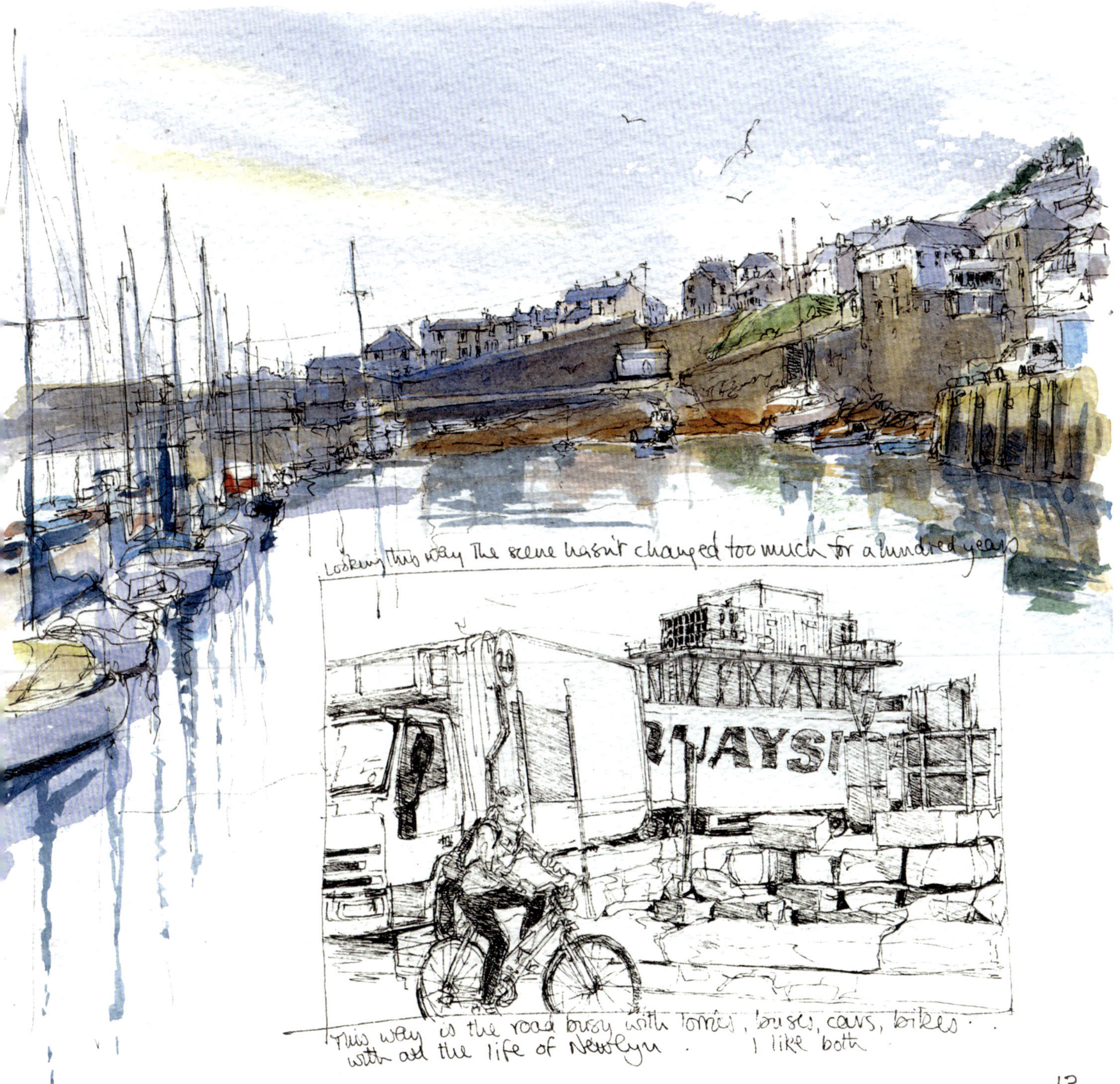
Looking this way the scene hasn't changed too much for a hundred years
DRINK
QUAYSI
This way is the road busy with lorries, buses, cars, bikes.
with all the life of Newlyn.   I like both

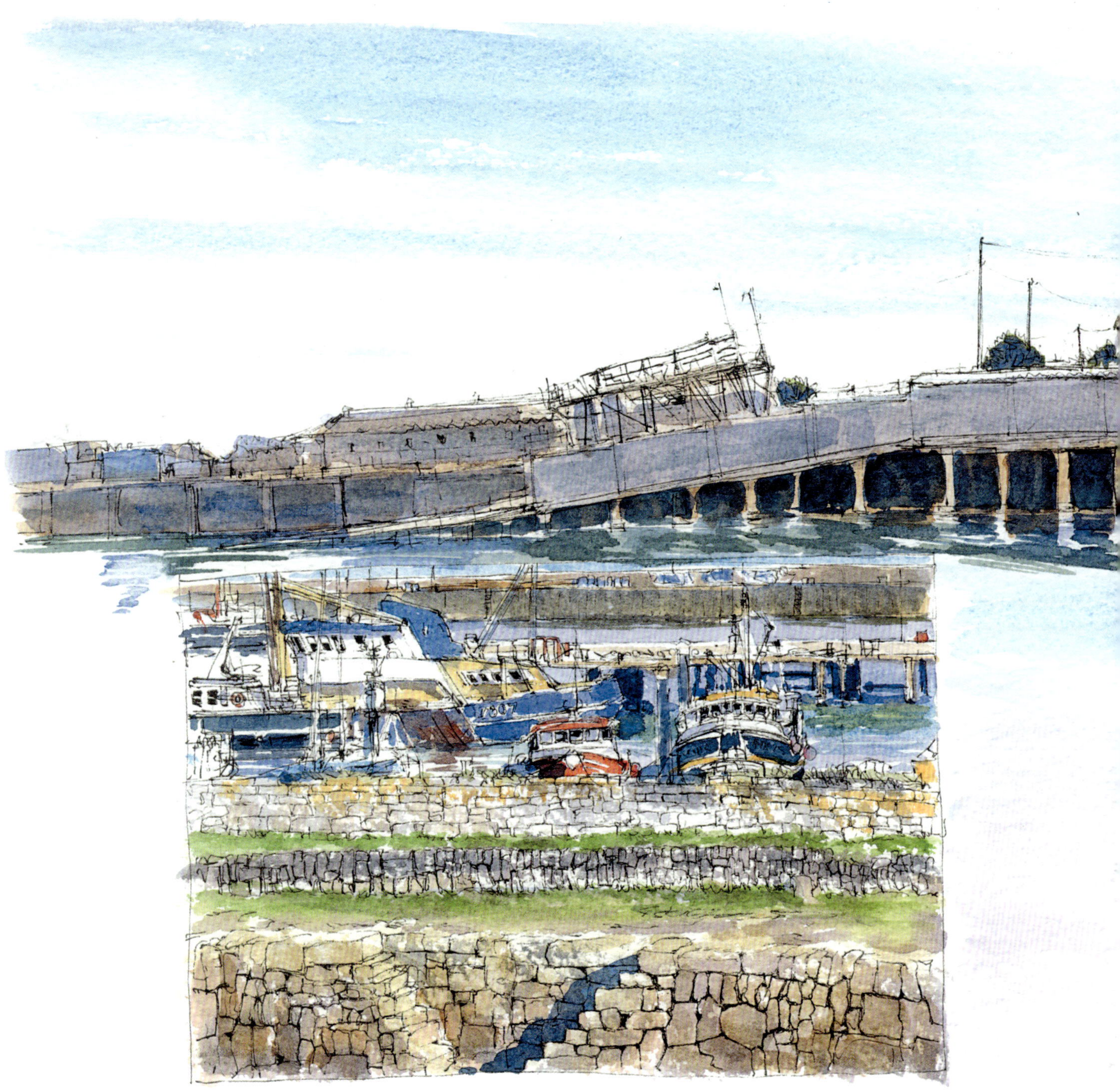

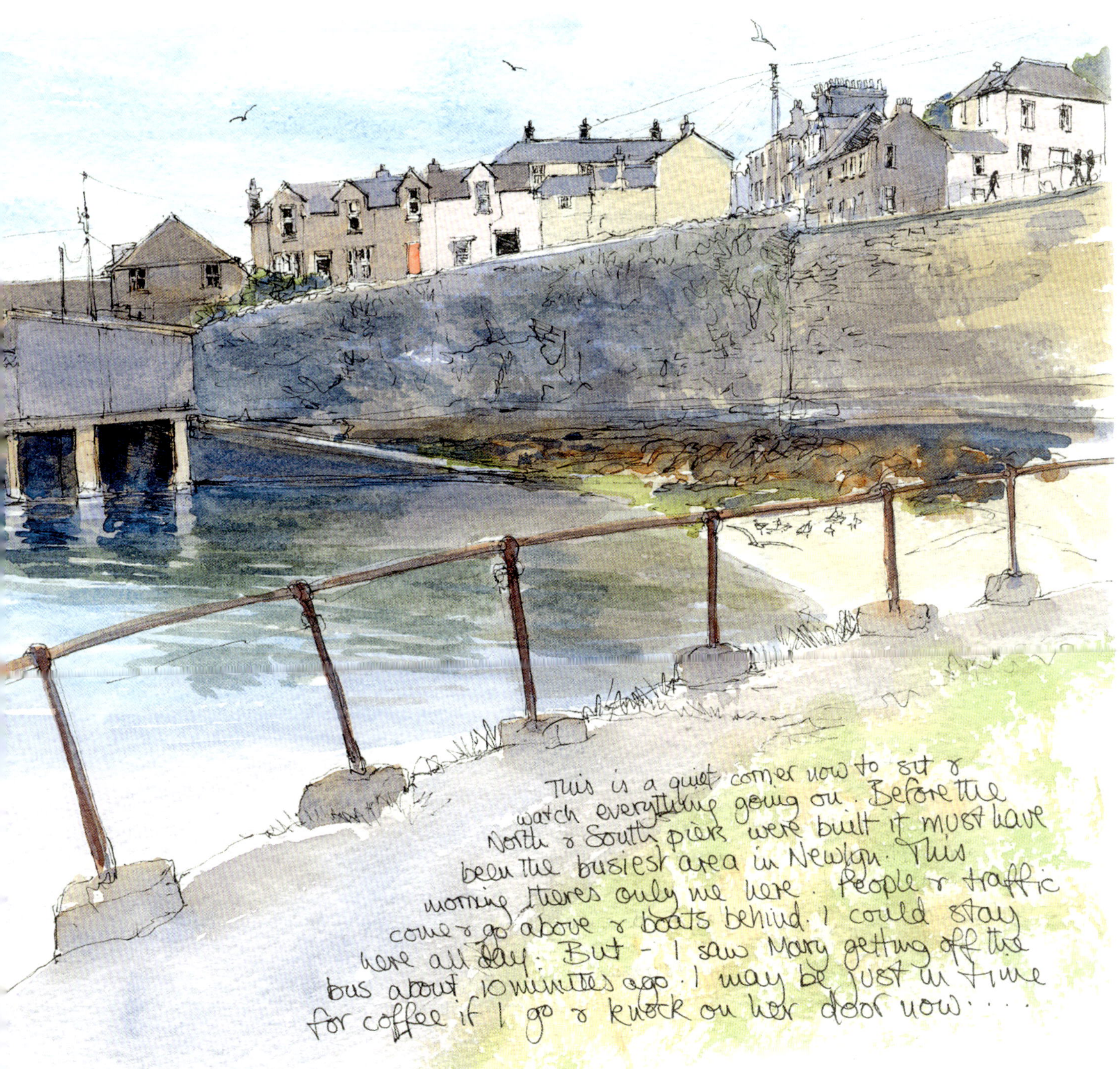

This is a quiet corner now to sit &
watch everything going on. Before the
North & South pier were built it must have
been the busiest area in Newlyn. This
morning theres only me here. People & traffic
come & go above & boats behind. I could stay
here all day. But — I saw Mary getting off the
bus about 10 minutes ago. I may be just in time
for coffee if I go & knock on her door now·····

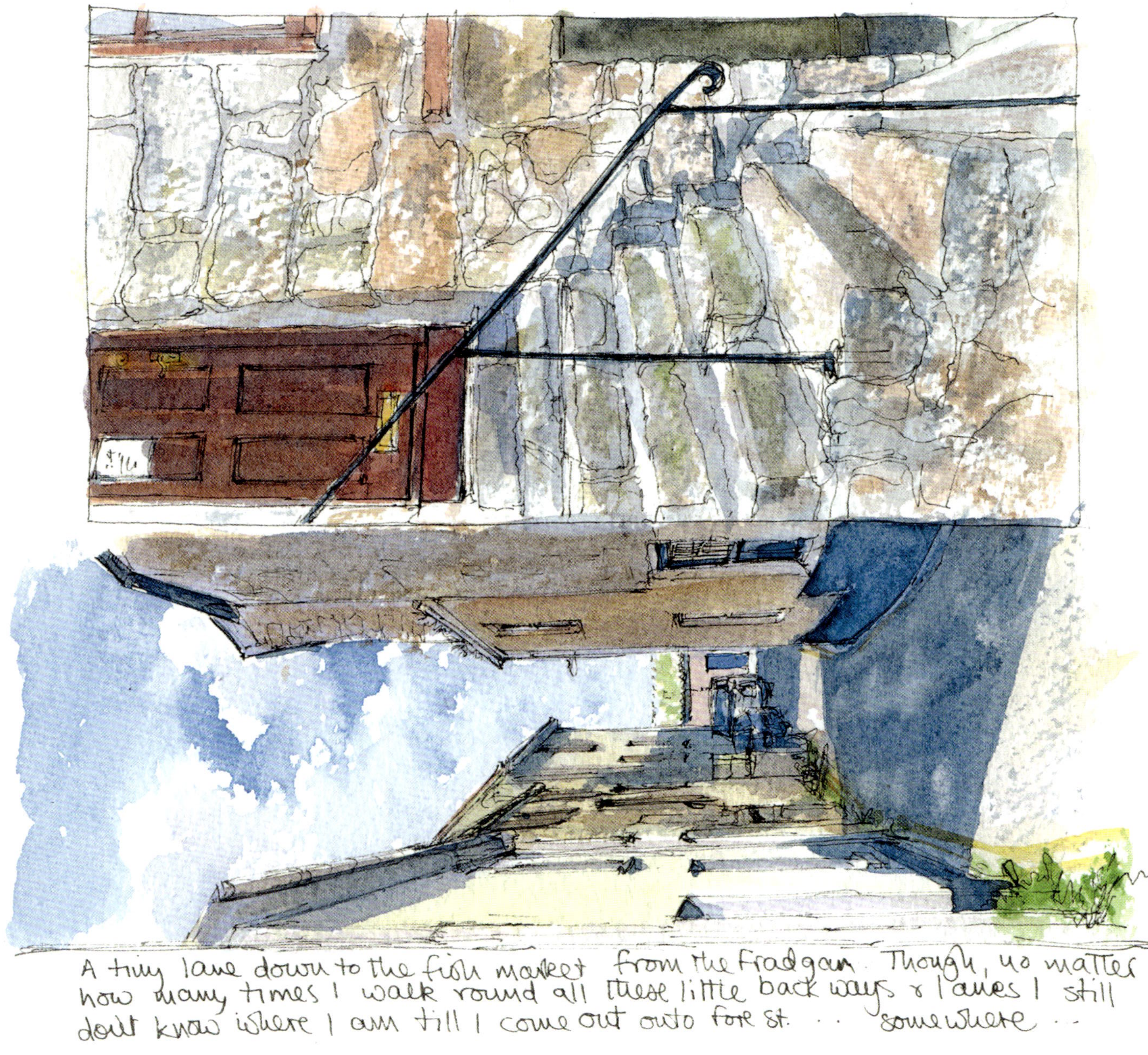

A tiny lane down to the fish market from the Fradgan. Though, no matter how many times I walk round all these little back ways & lanes I still don't know where I am till I come out onto fore st. . . somewhere . .

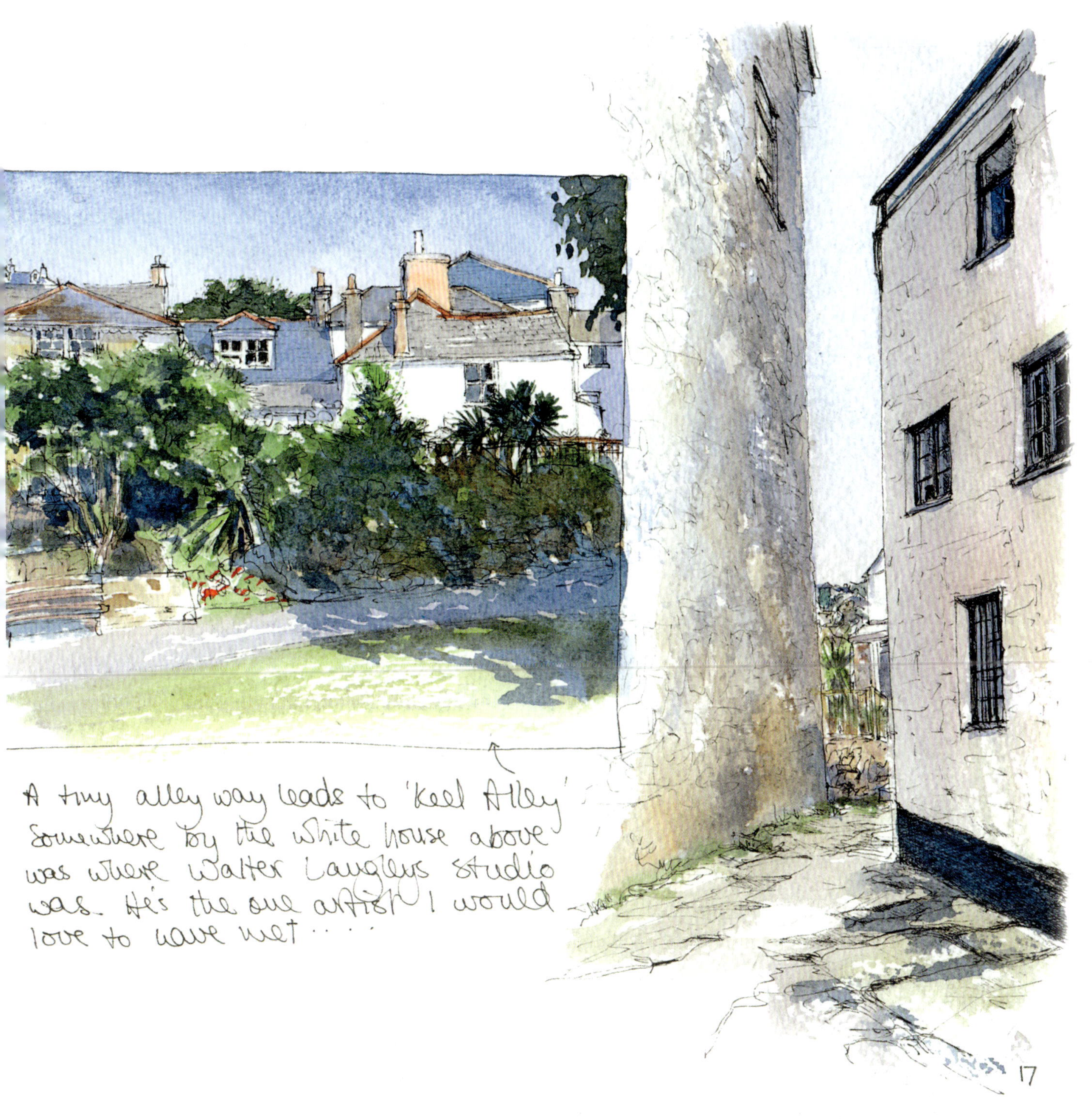

A tiny alley way leads to 'Keel Alley'
Somewhere by the white house above
was where Walter Langleys studio
was. He's the one artist I would
love to have met ....

17

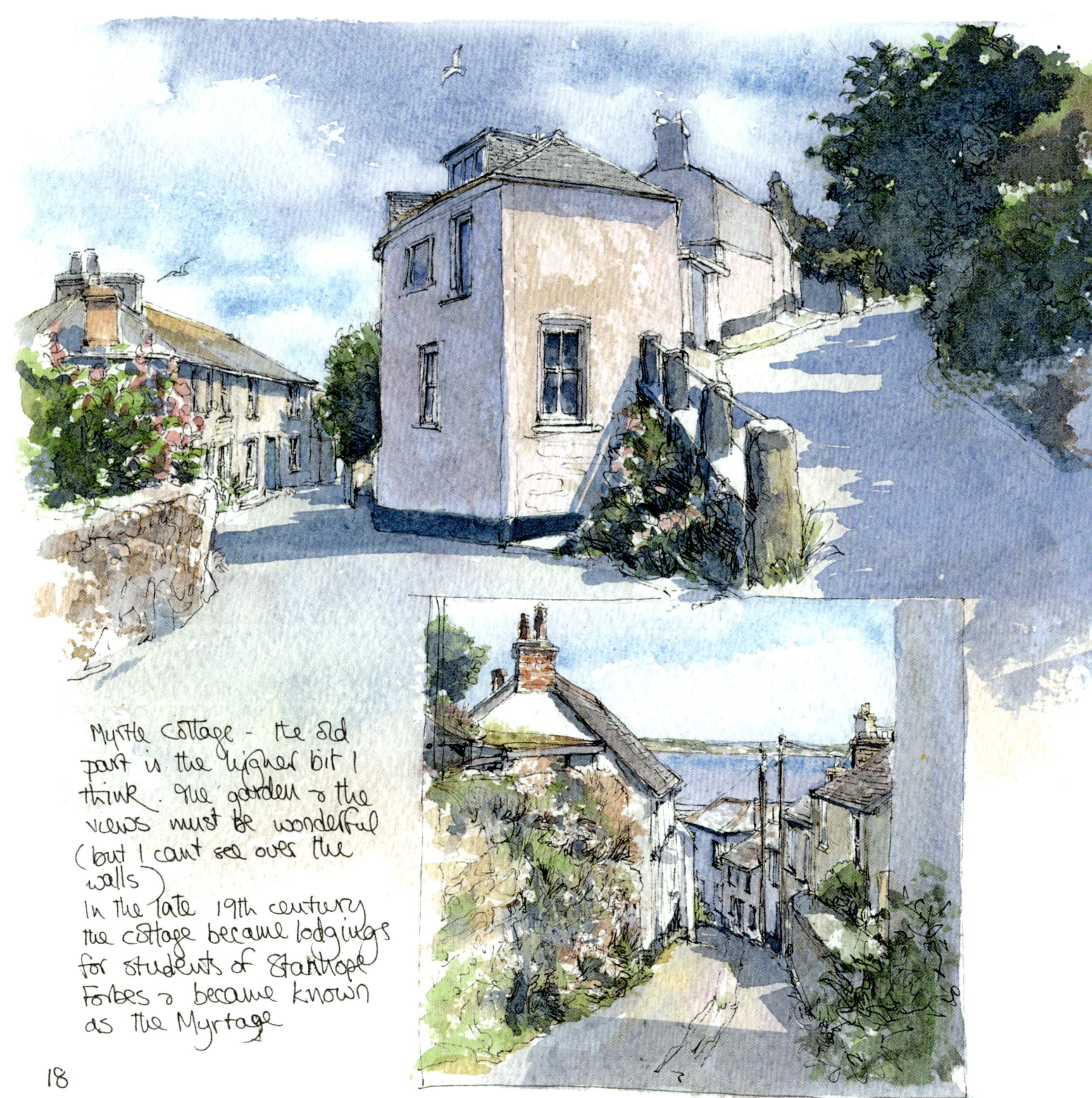

Myrtle Cottage - the old
part is the higher bit I
think. The garden & the
views must be wonderful
(but I cant see over the
walls)
In the late 19th century
the cottage became lodgings
for students of Stanhope
Forbes & became known
as the Myrtage

18

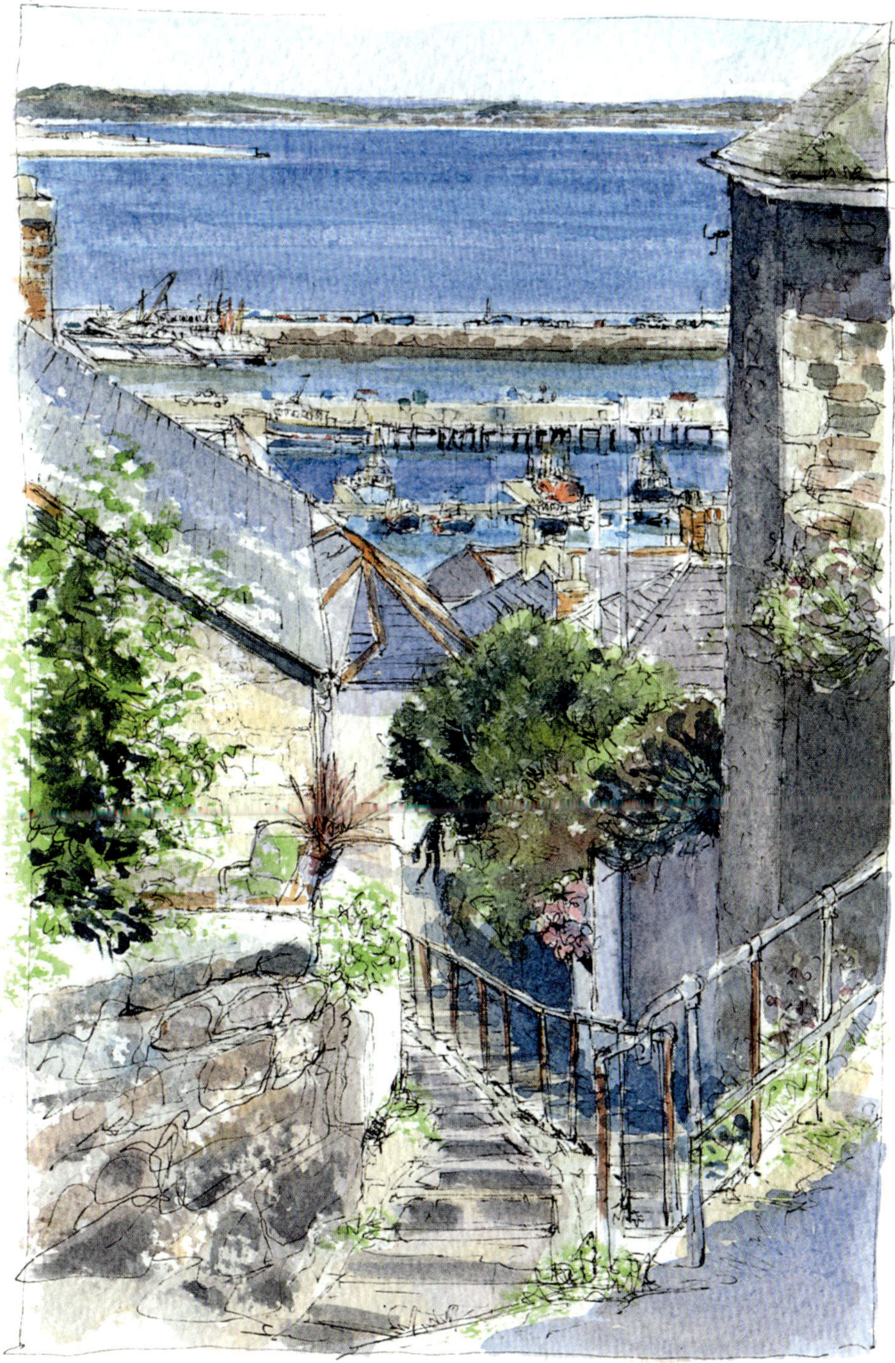

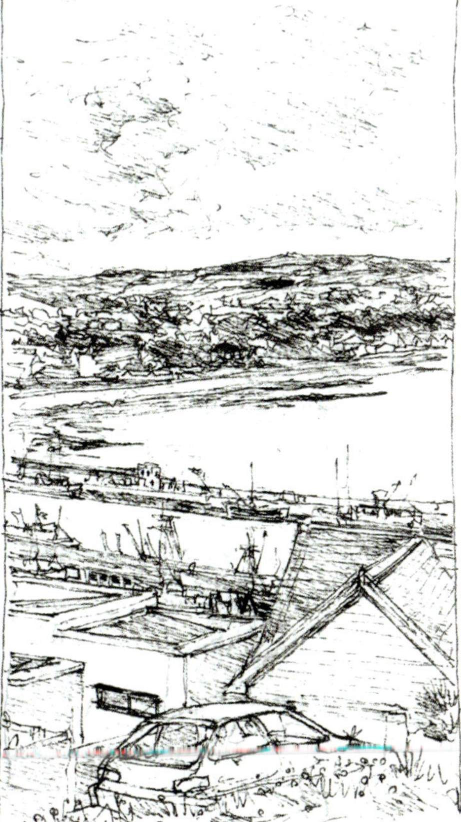

Even higher up the hill....
The views are great from
up here. And I have to
stop often to look.

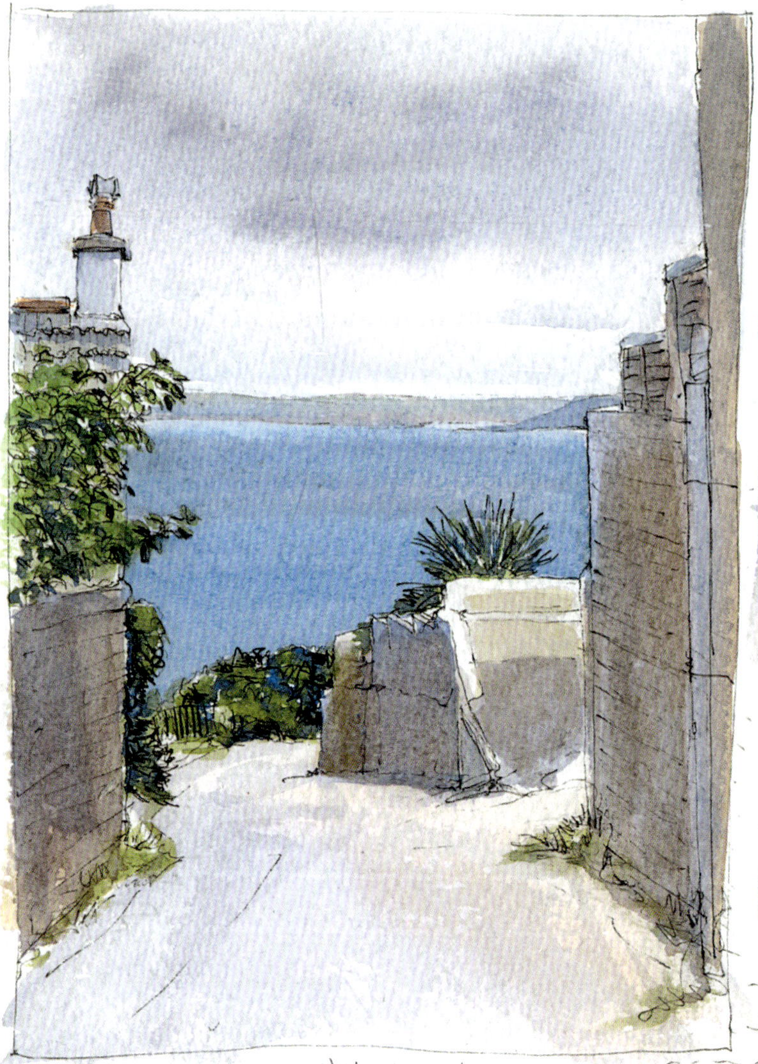

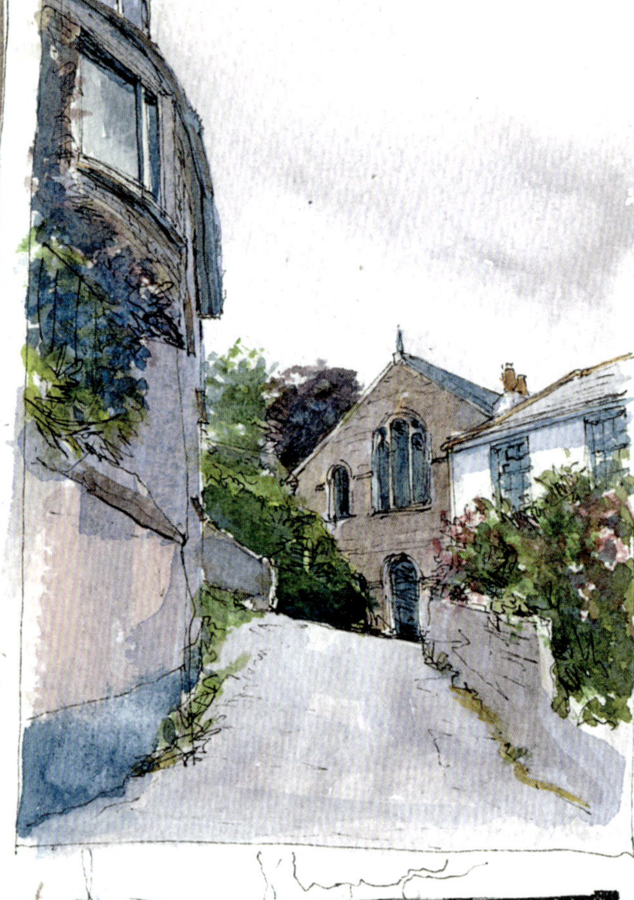

Looking down Bowjey Hill. It is steep.
I lean backwards as I go down. So far
I haven't tried coming up this way.

I like the indecision
of this road sign …
r the angle of the road

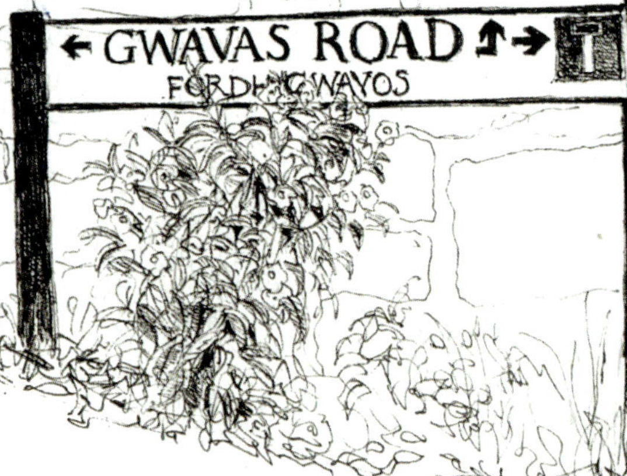

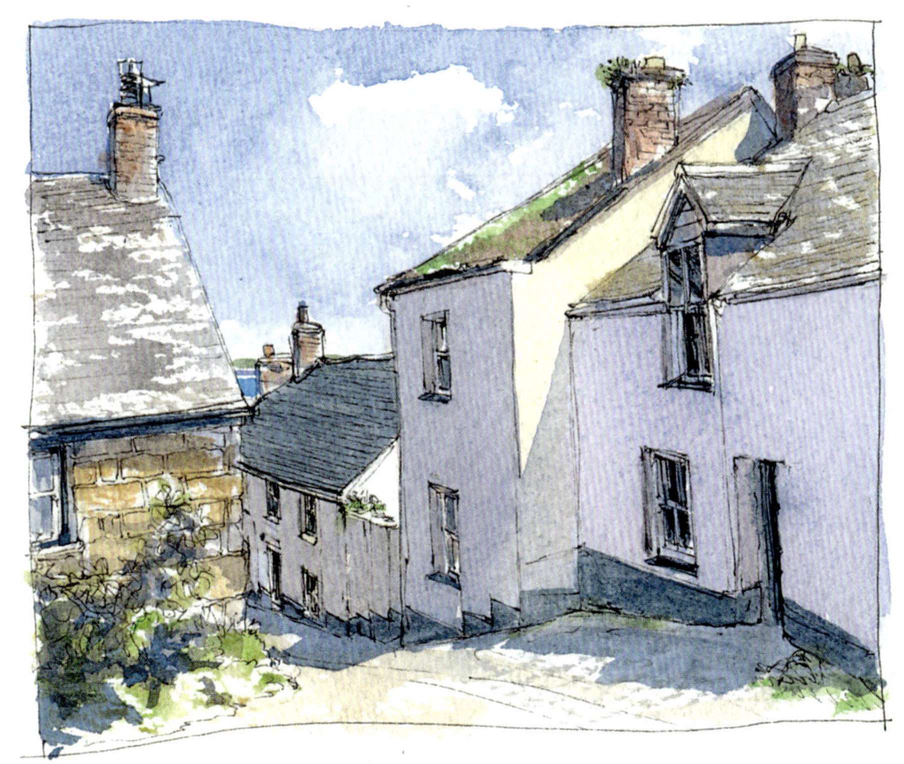

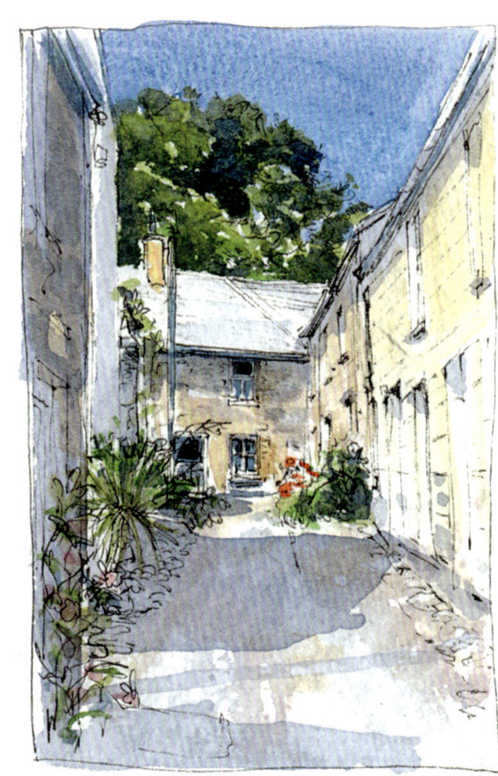

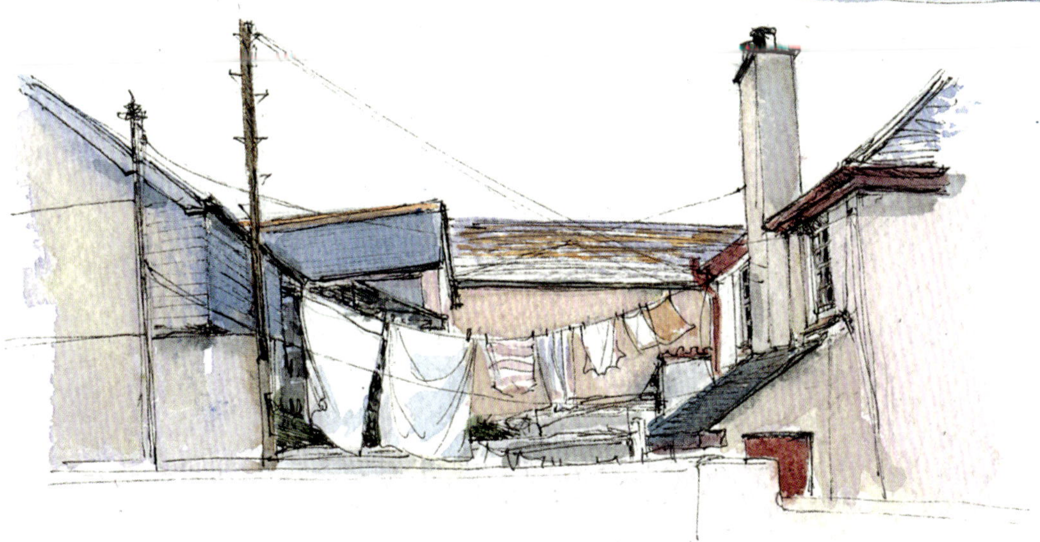

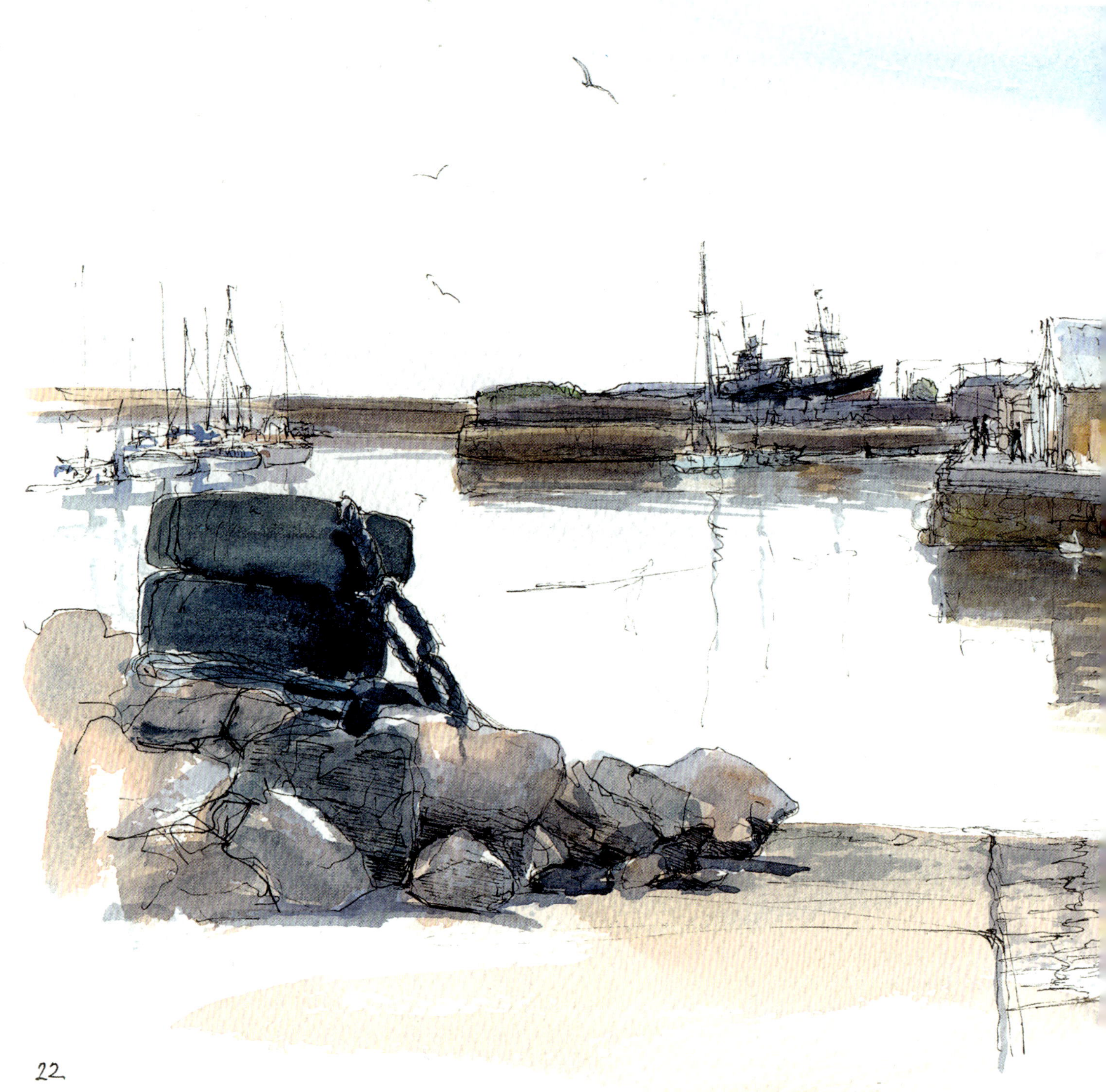

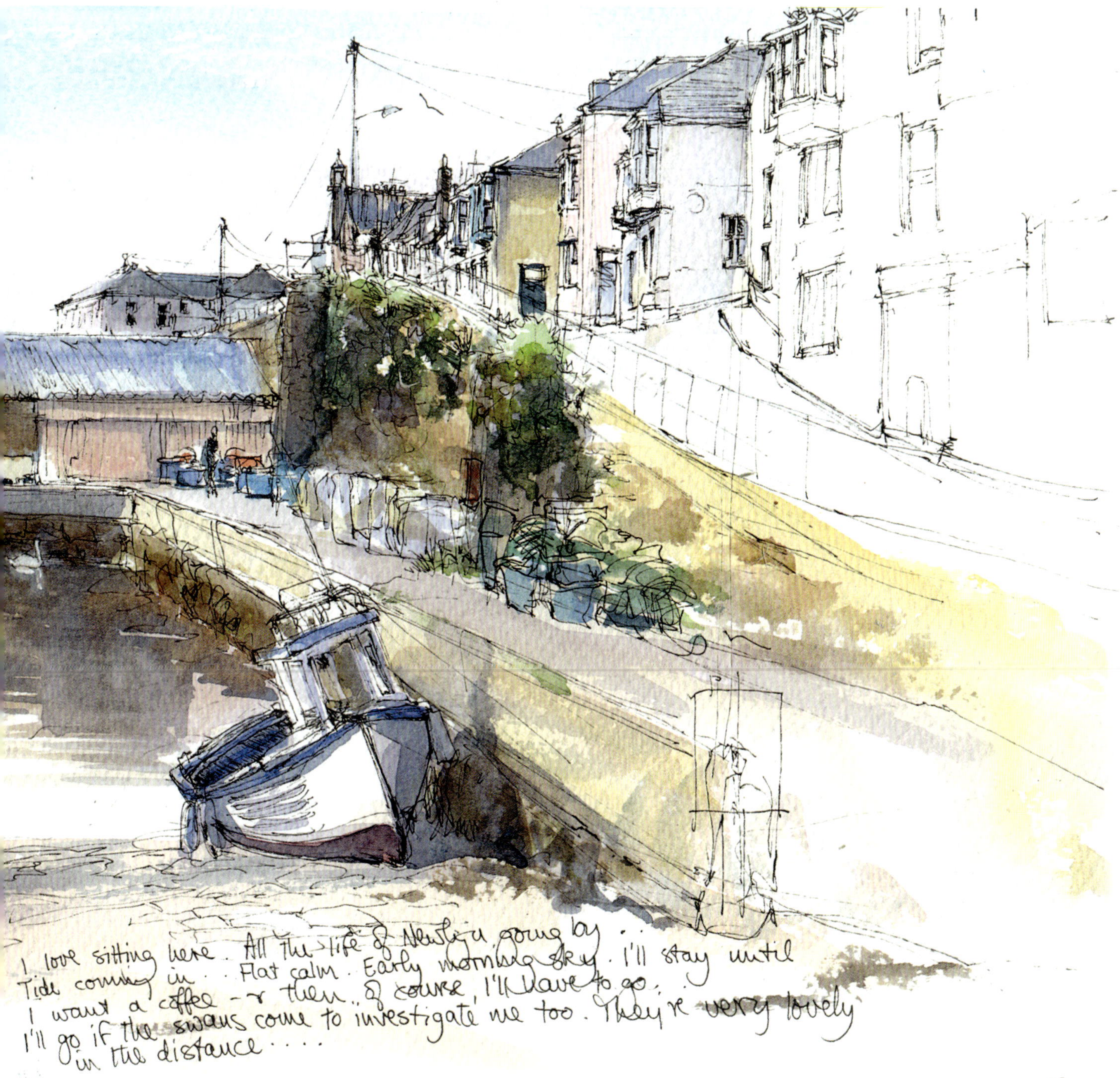
I love sitting here. All the life of Newlyn going by...
Tide coming in... Flat calm. Early morning sky. I'll stay until
I want a coffee — r then... & course, I'll have to go...
I'll go if the swans come to investigate me too. They're very lovely
in the distance....

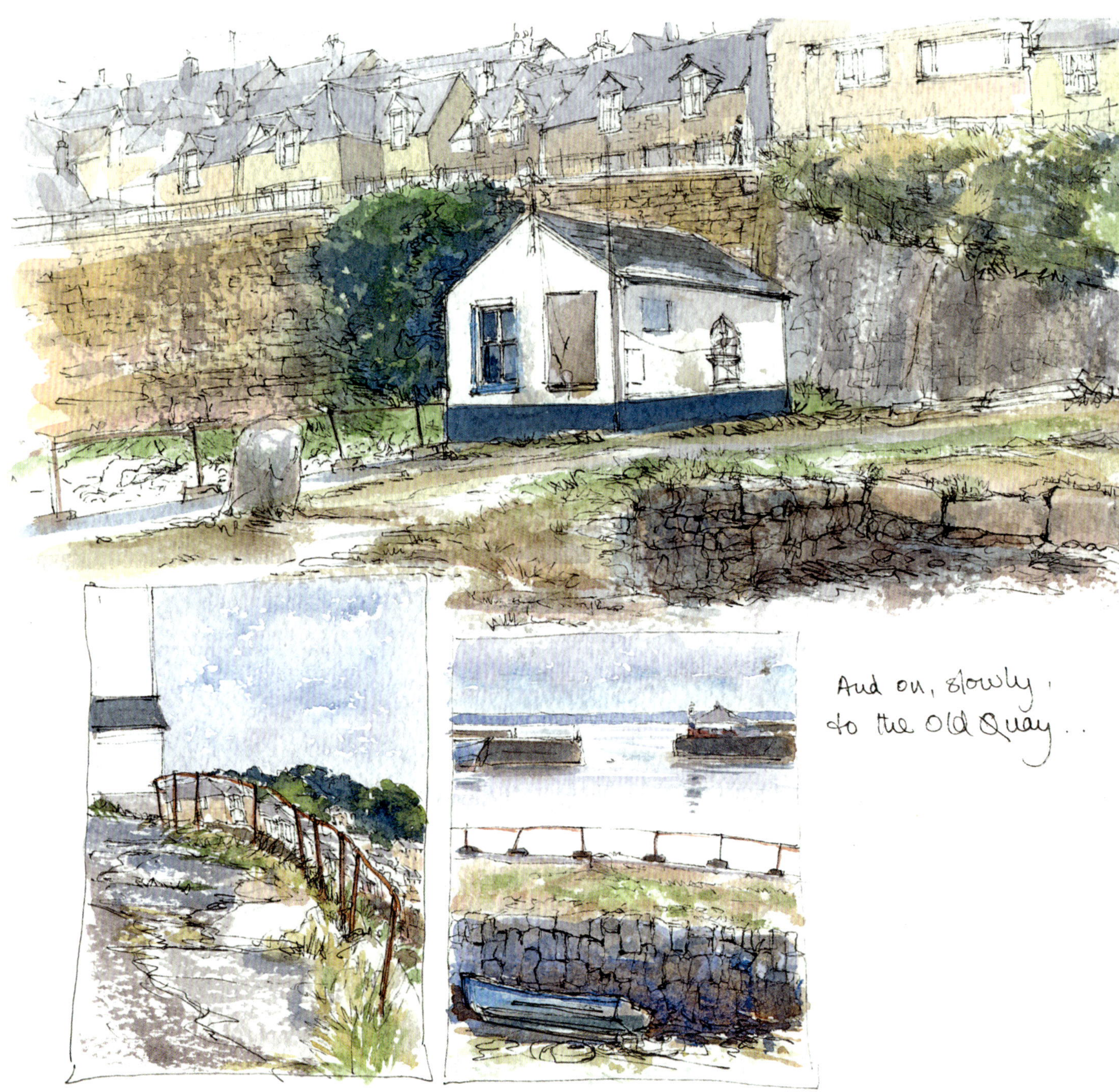

And on, slowly,
to the Old Quay...

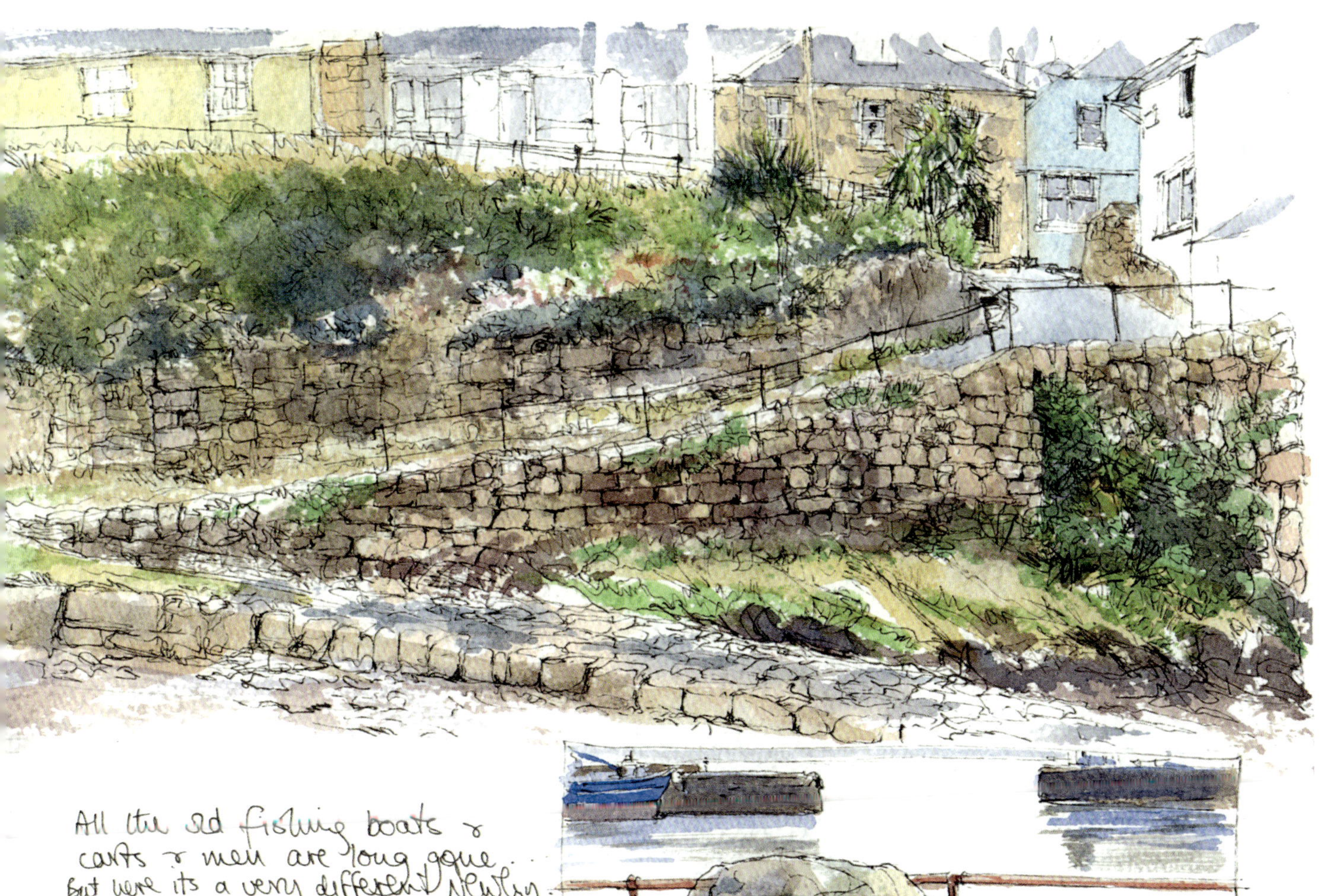

All the old fishing boats & carts & men are long gone.. But here its a very different Newlyn. still.

The quay wall used to carry on around where the railings are now. Sitting here I realise that its where some of the Newlyn school paintings are set. looking out for return'g boats in rough seas, before the South Pier was built . . .

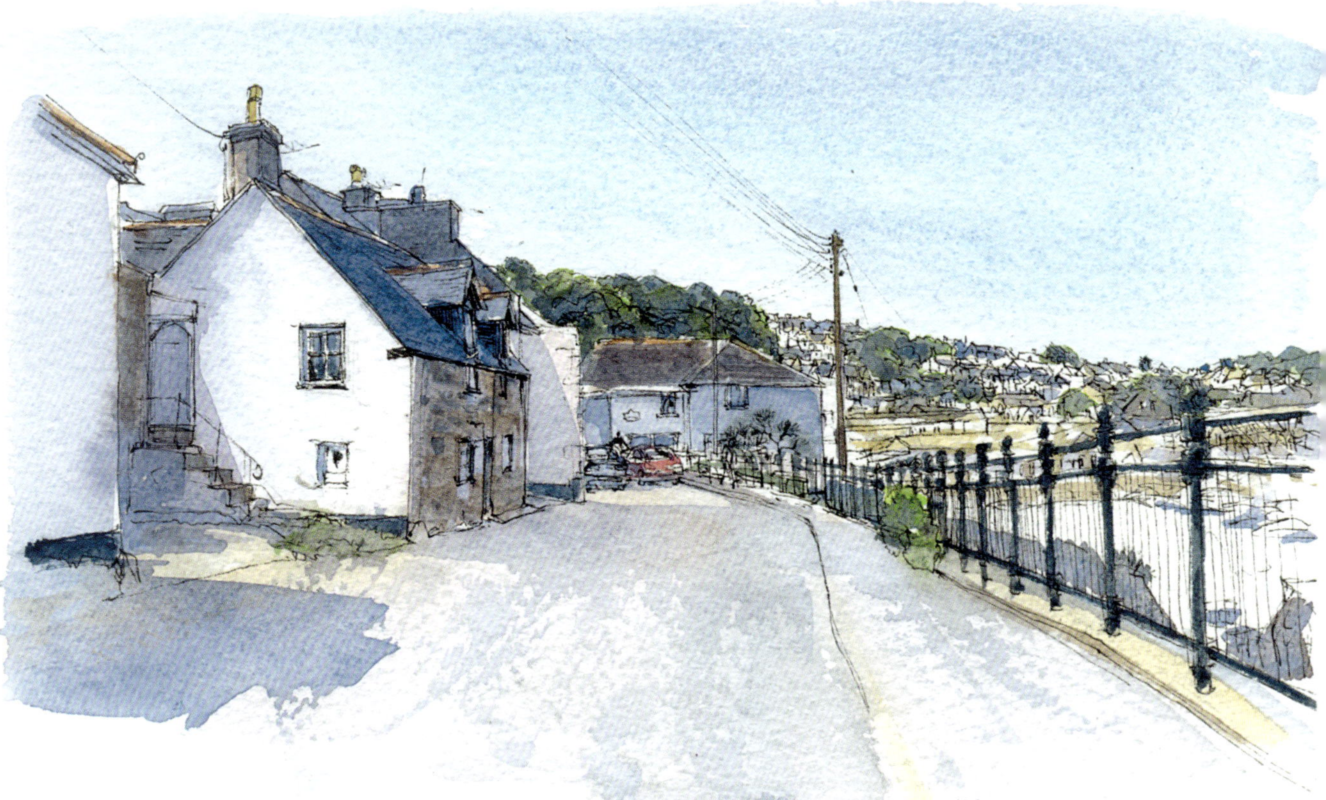

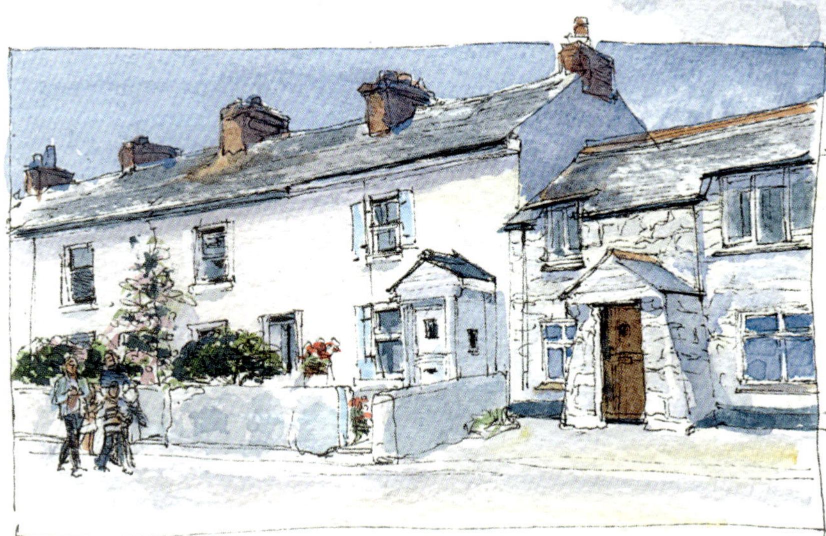

opposite ends of the town.
This is Tolcarne. I said
I'd put Mikki's cat in
the book because he always
sits on the tables outside
the Tolcarne.... Only —
not when I walk by.
Her house looks lovely
with all the roses
though....

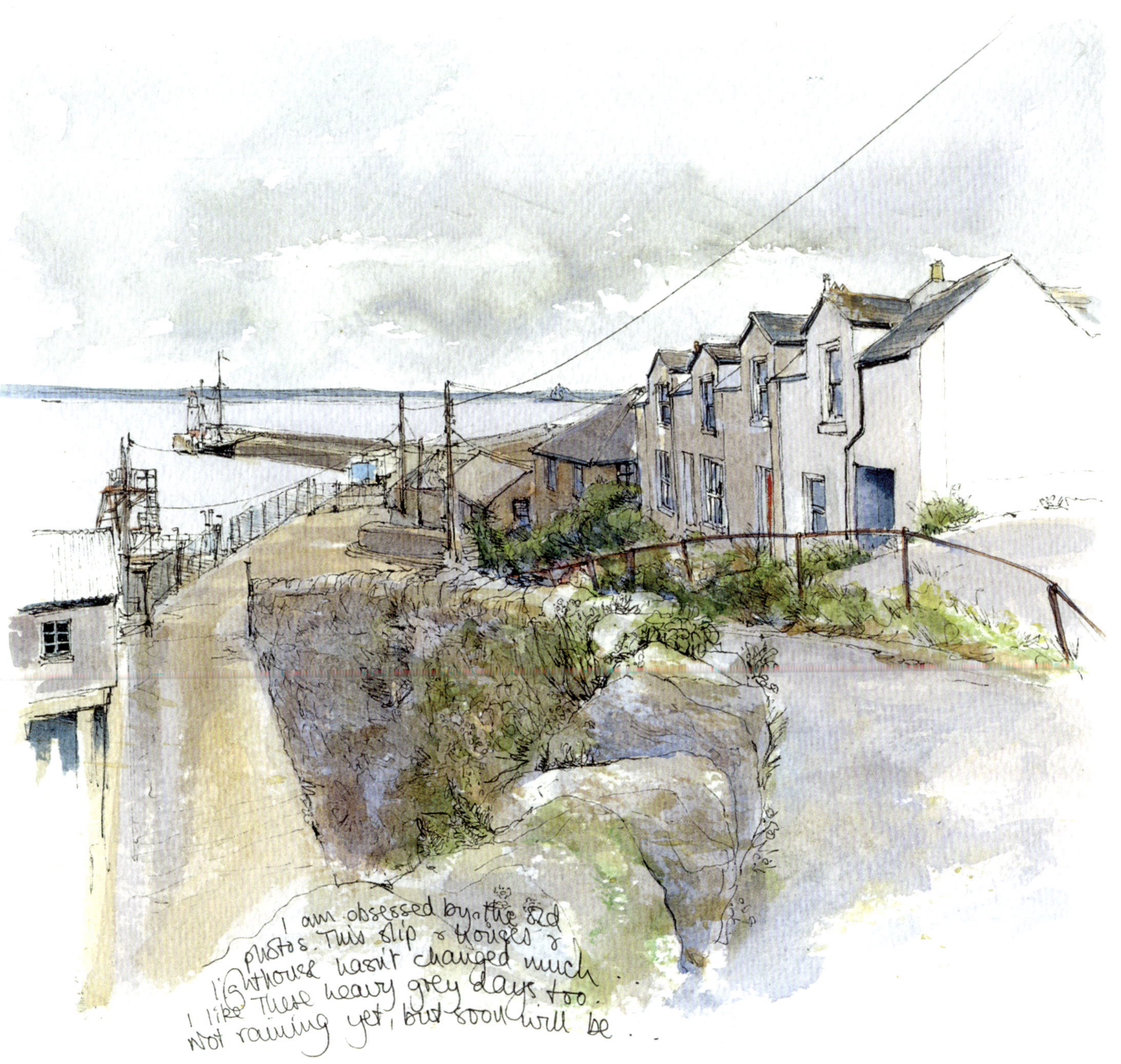

I am obsessed by the old
photos. This slip & houses &
lighthouse hasn't changed much.
I like these heavy grey days too.
Not raining yet, but soon will be.

27

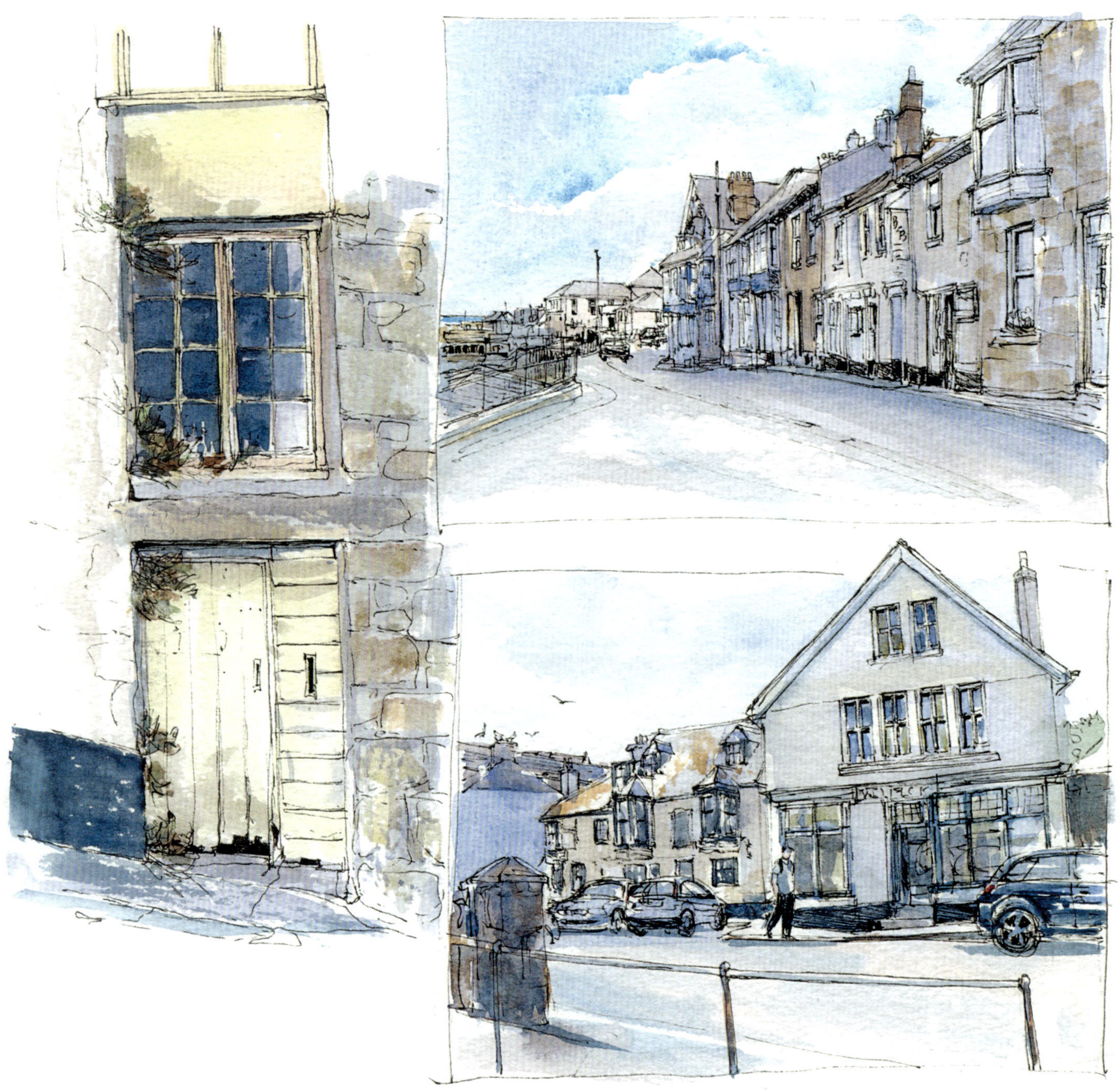

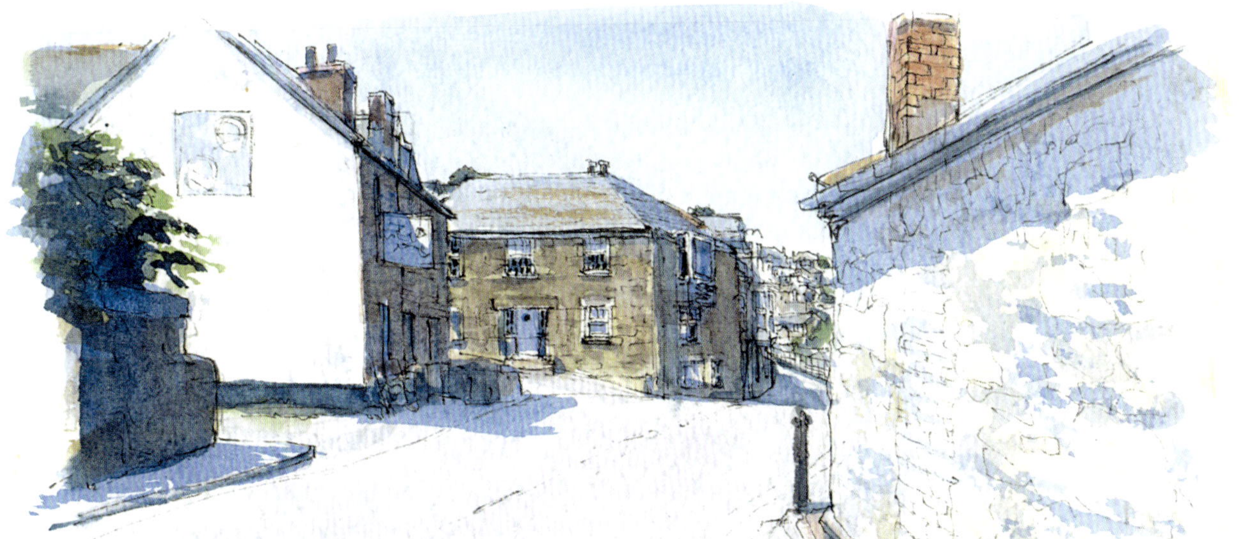

I think this is where the old 'fishermen's rest' was.

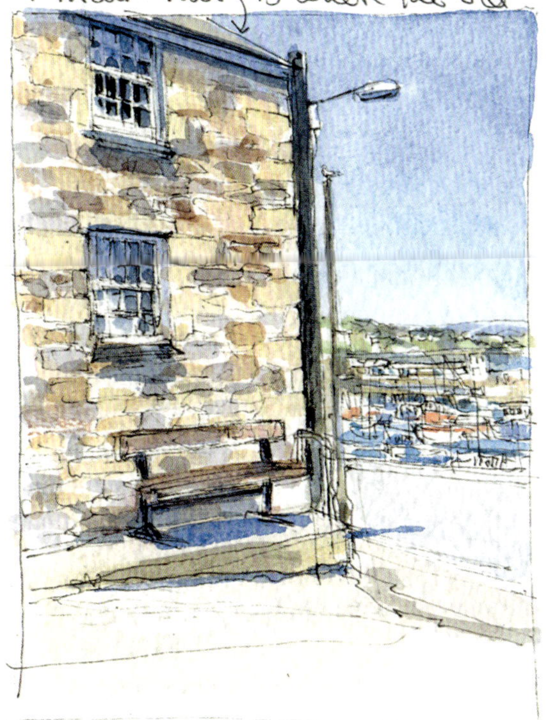

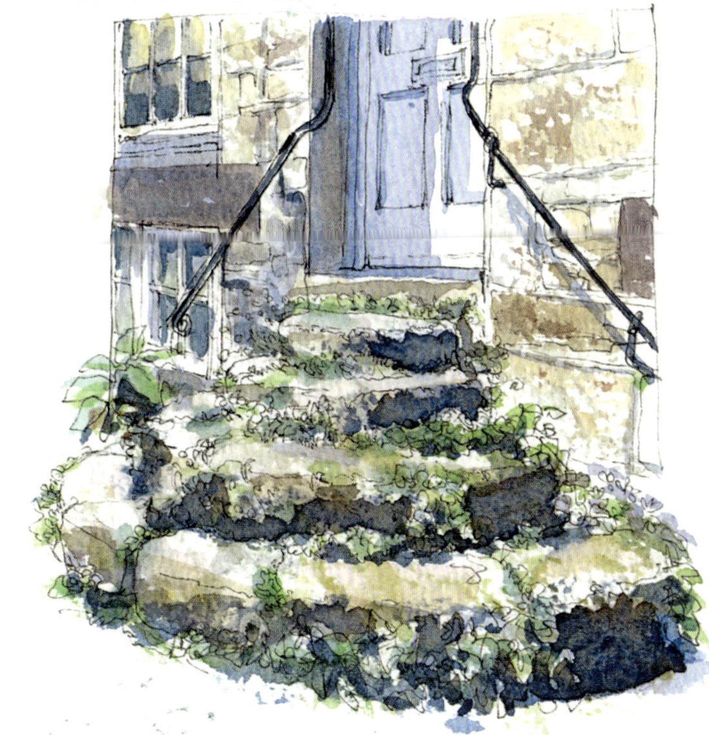

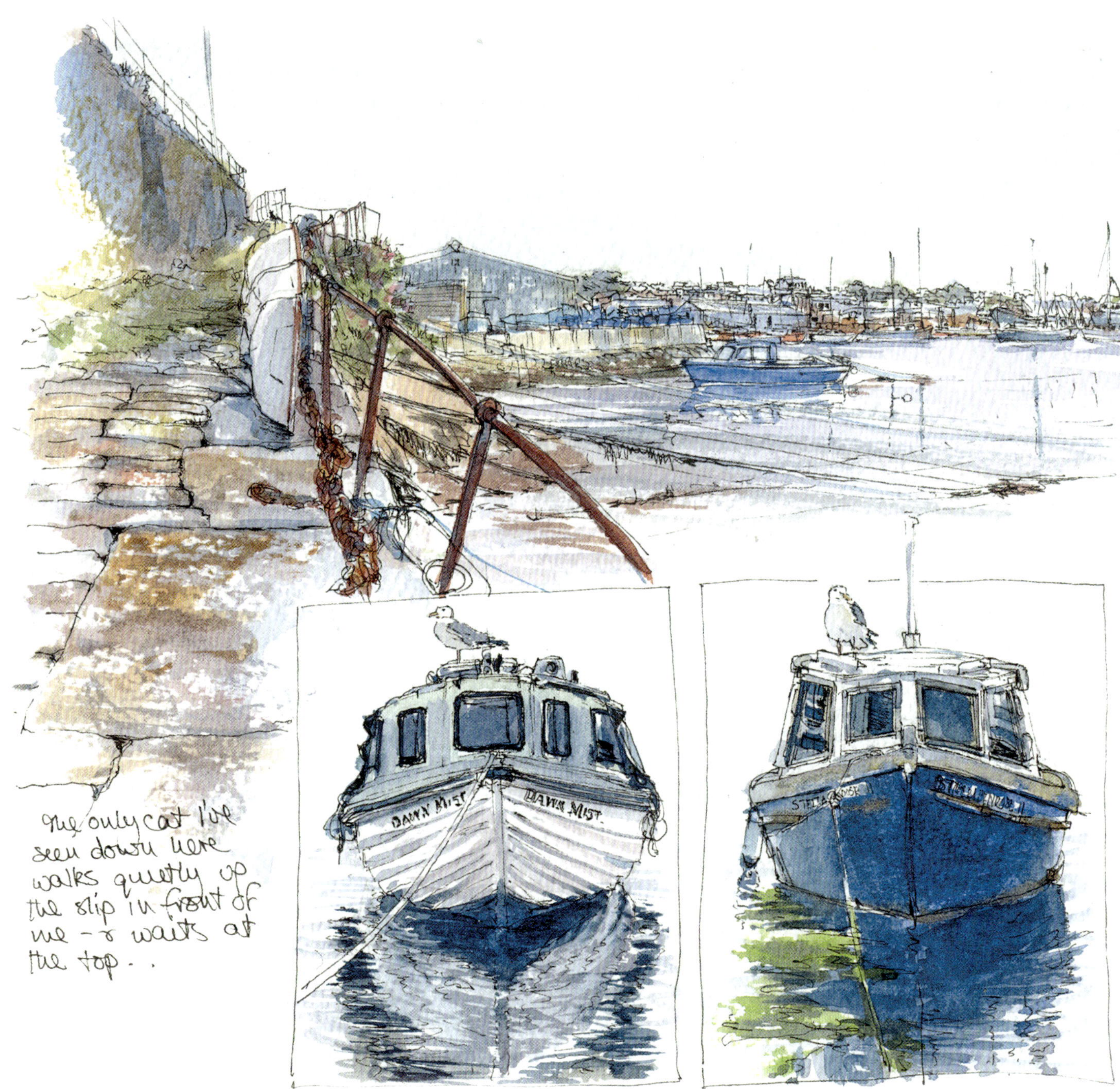

The only cat I've
seen down here
walks quietly up
the slip in front of
me — & waits at
the top . .

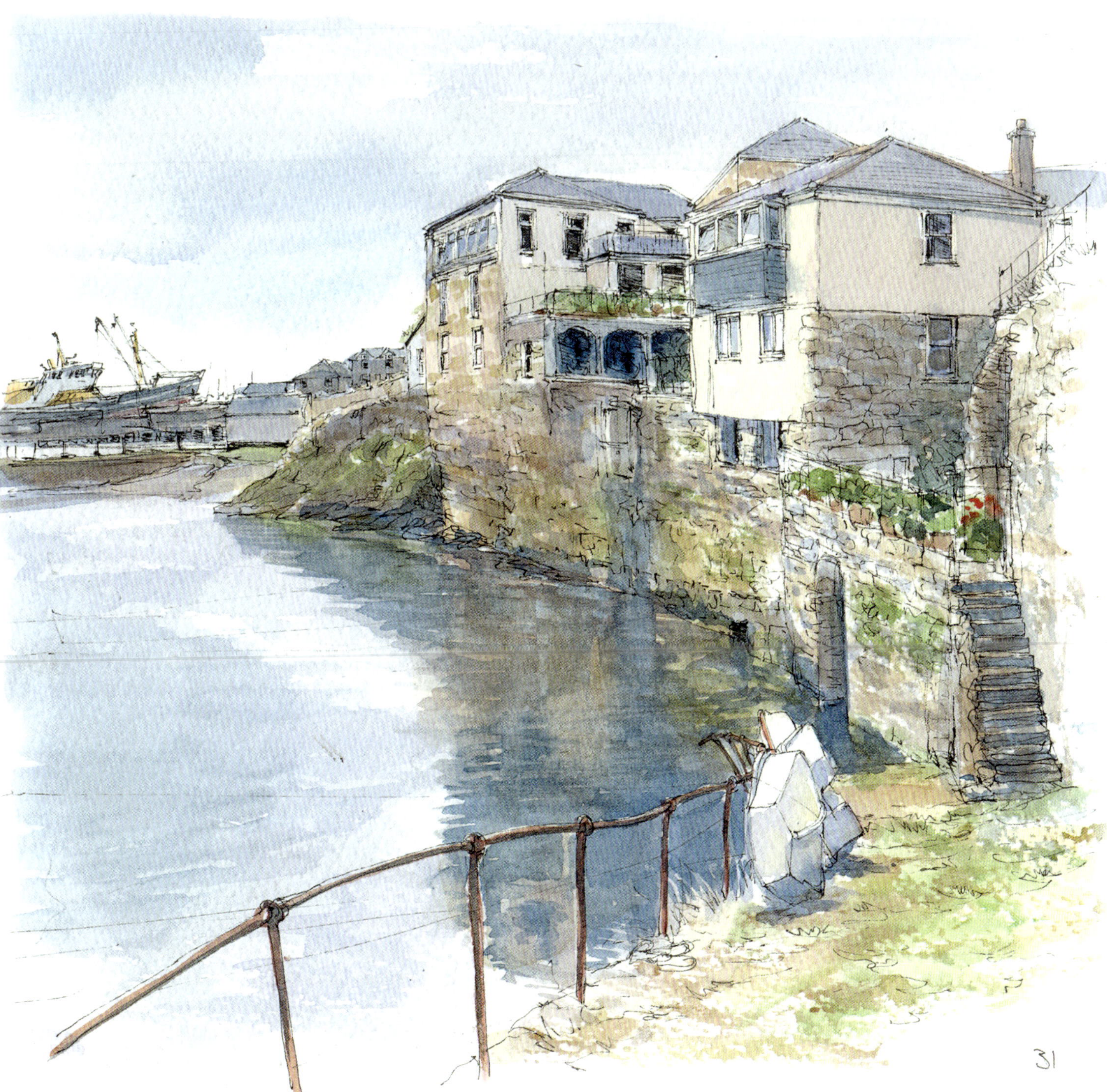

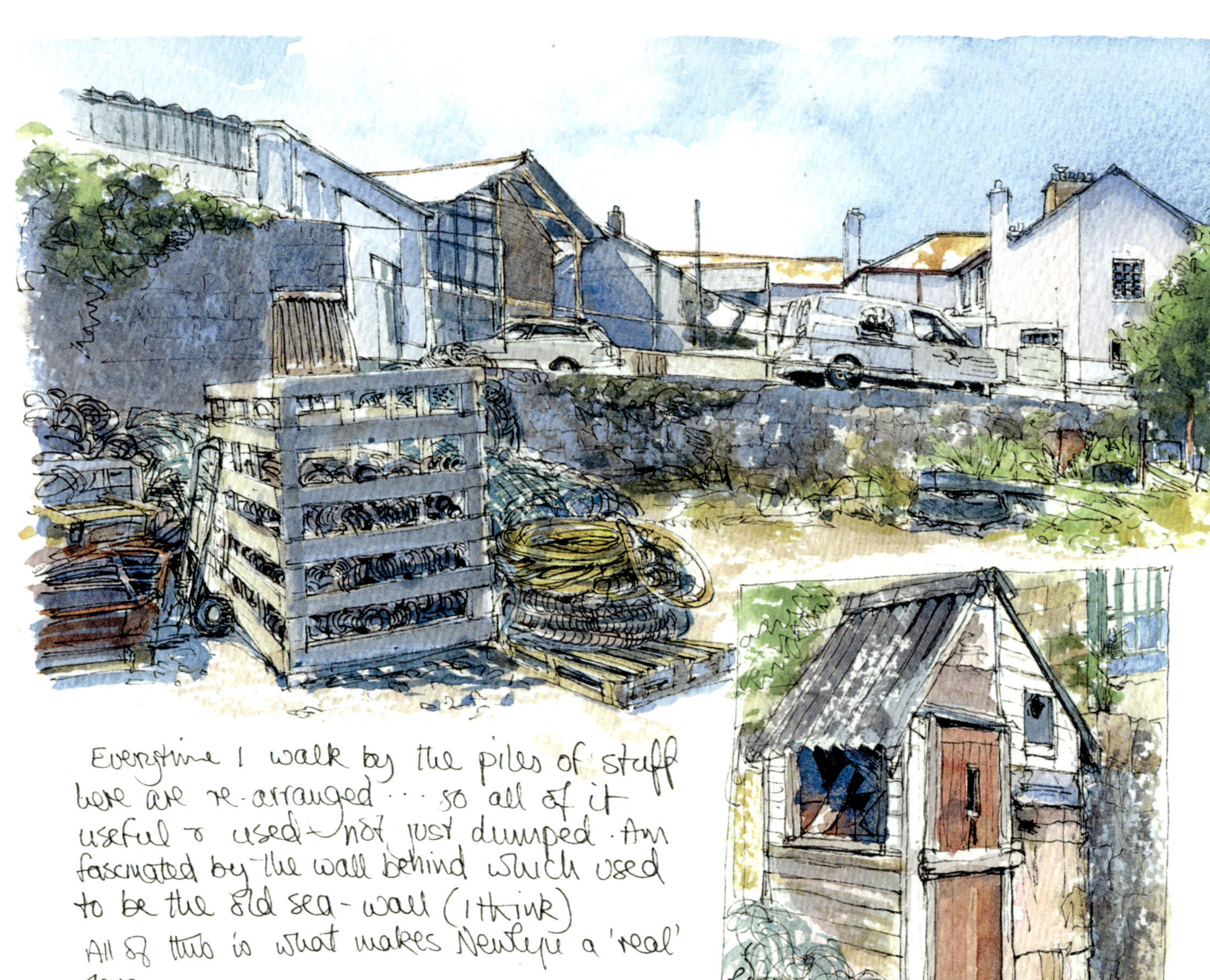

Everytime I walk by the piles of stuff
here are re-arranged... so all of it
useful & used—not just dumped. Am
fascinated by the wall behind which used
to be the old sea-wall (I think)
All of this is what makes Newlyn a 'real'
place ...

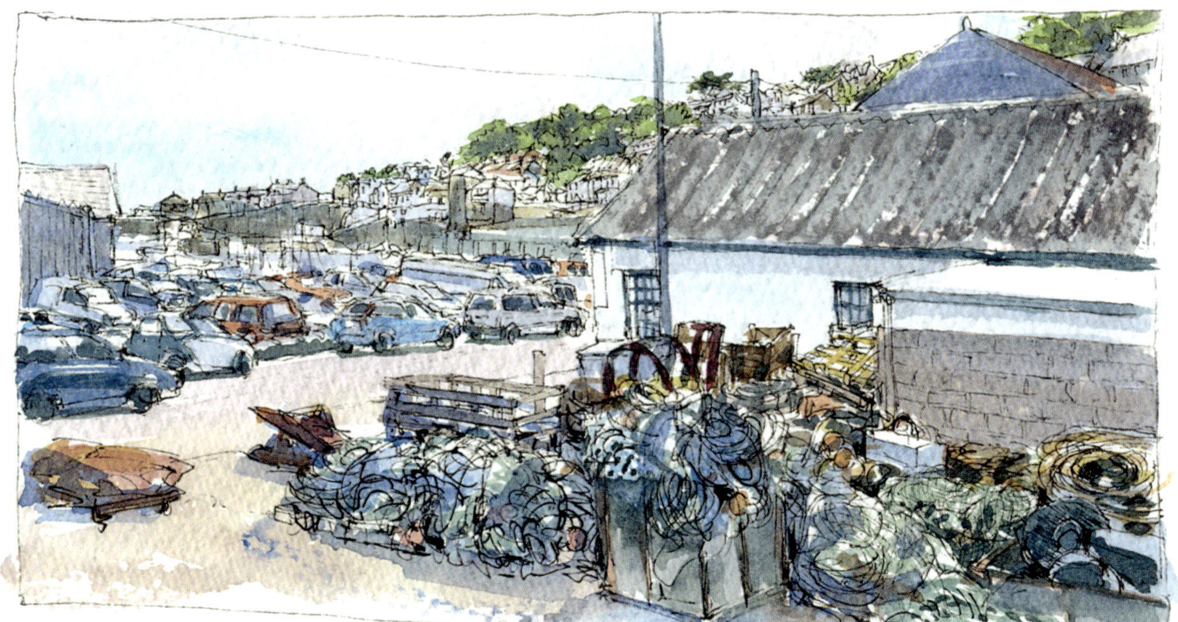

All this - car park, harbour buildings, road, all the buildings here ↑ all on land reclaimed from the sea.

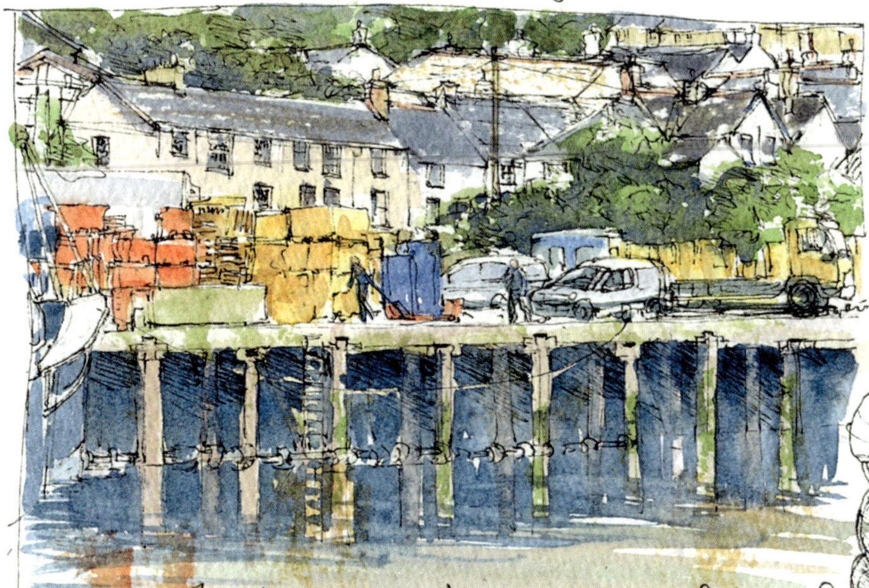

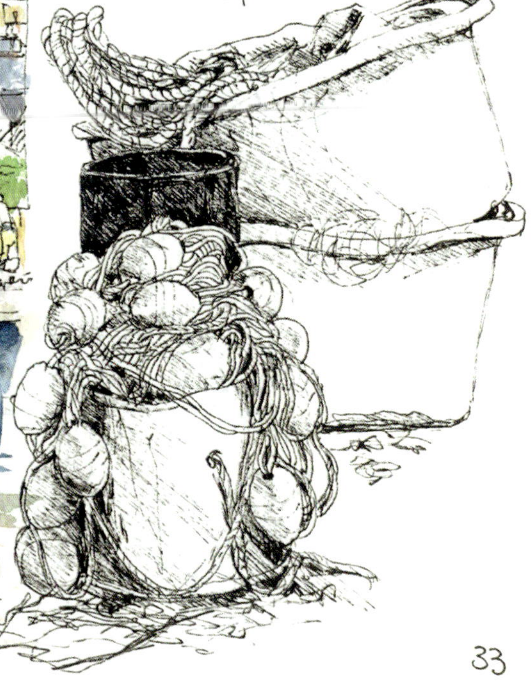

& this looks back over the re-claimed land to what used to be Gwavas quay.

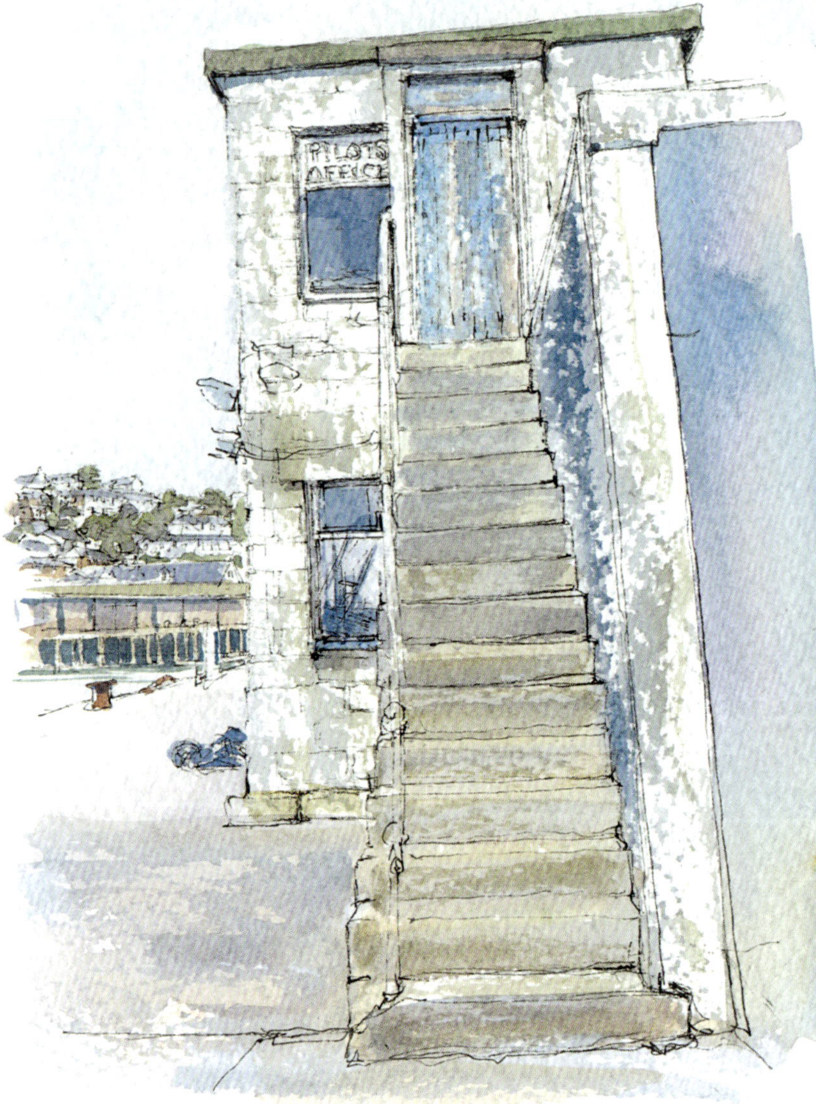

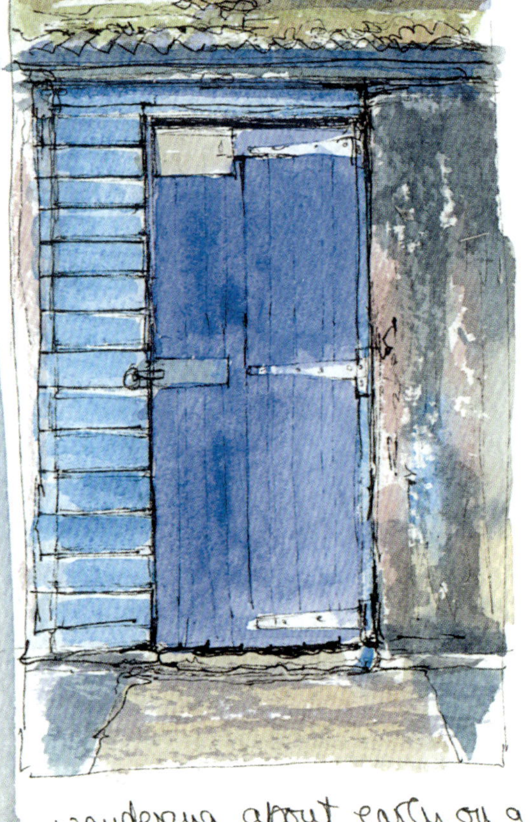

wandering about early on a
Sunday morning. No forklifts
or lorries rushing about, but
some men working as usual.
I asked what time the
market starts - 5.30 am ish -
so thats going to be an early
morning then (sorry - I never
did get there.)

I also asked where would be a good place to stand when its
busy so that I didn't get in the way. 'That corners where the
artists usually stand' he said......

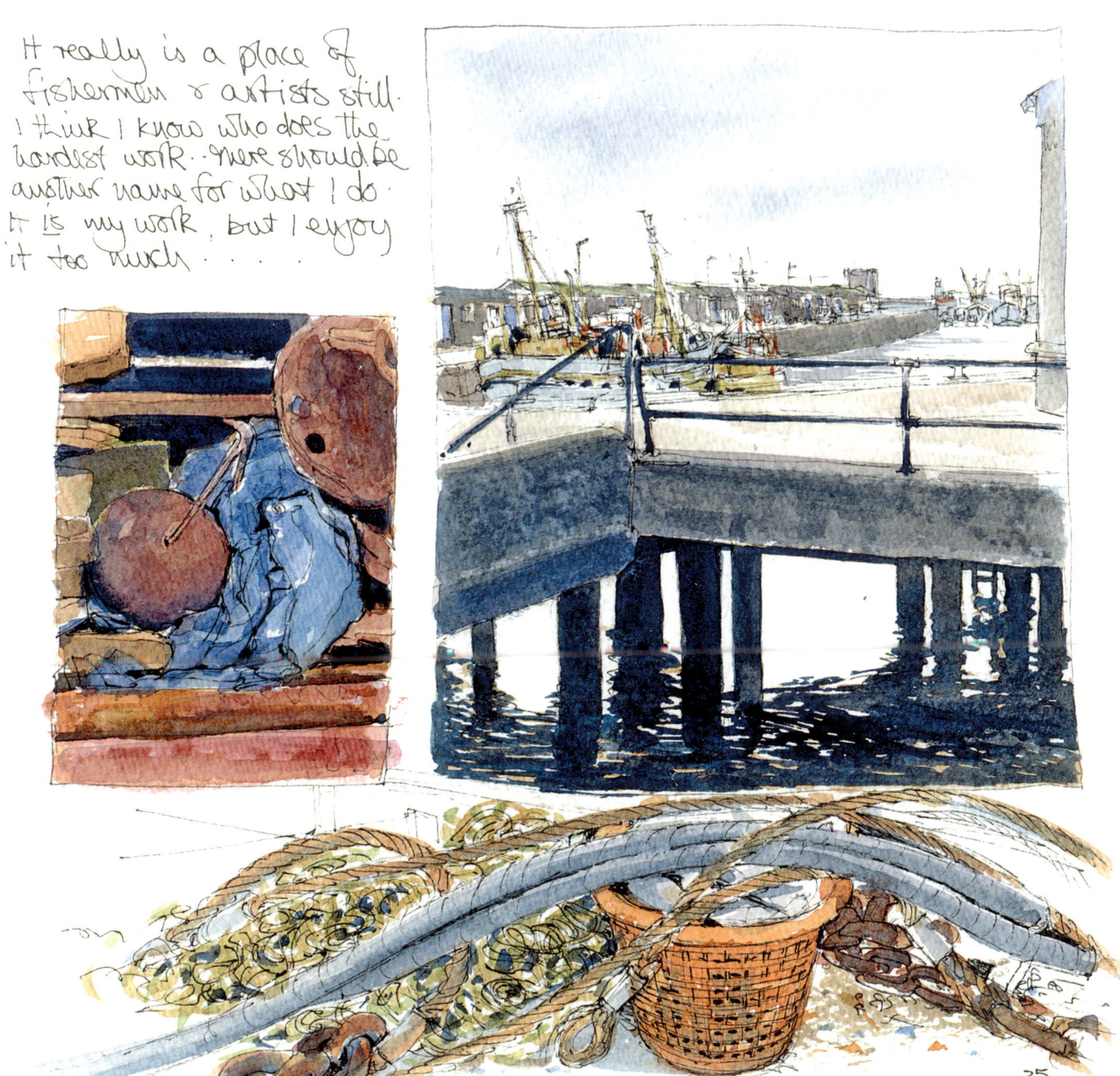

It really is a place of
fishermen & artists still.
I think I know who does the
hardest work. There should be
another name for what I do.
It is my work, but I enjoy
it too much . . . .

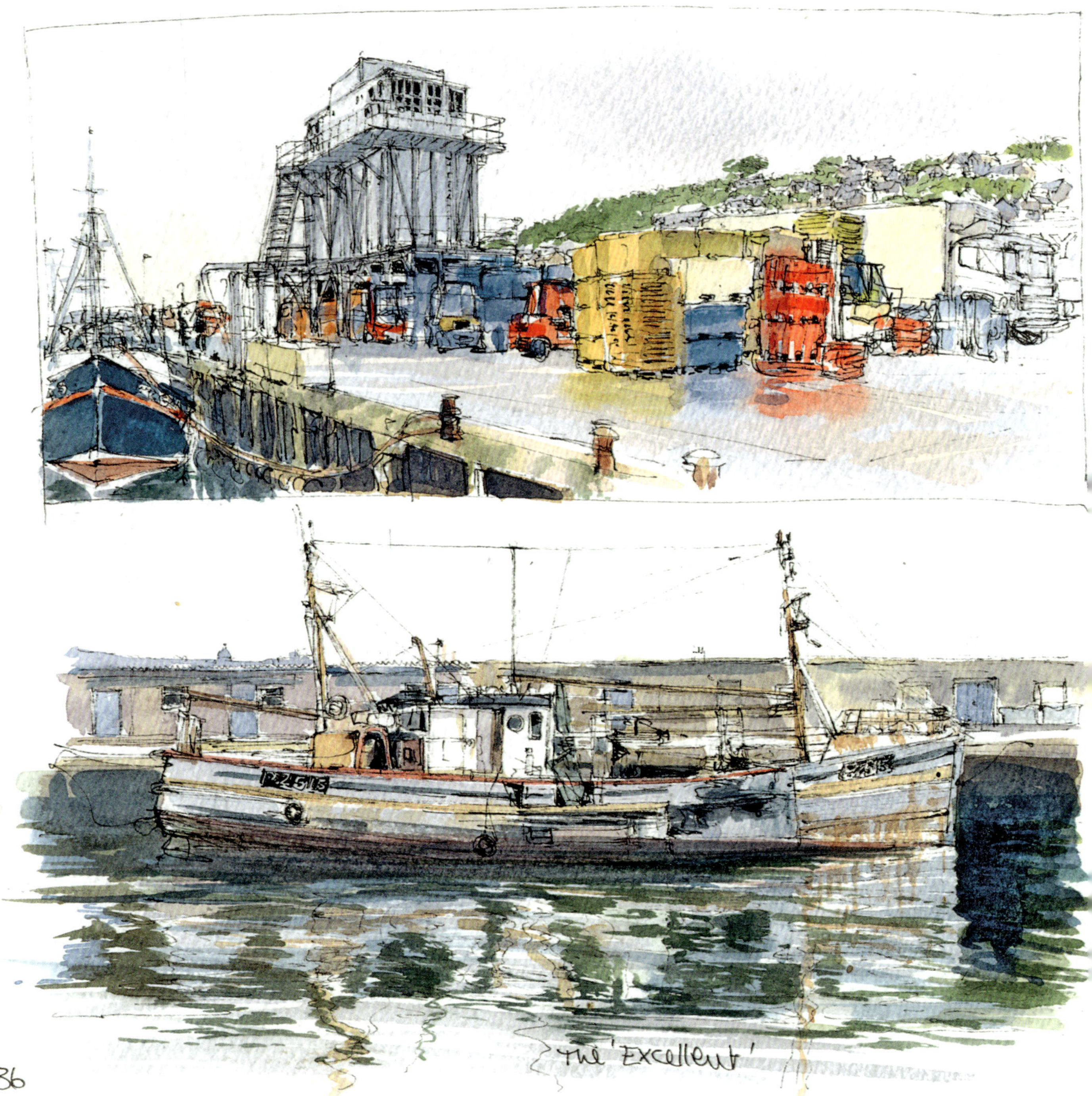

36

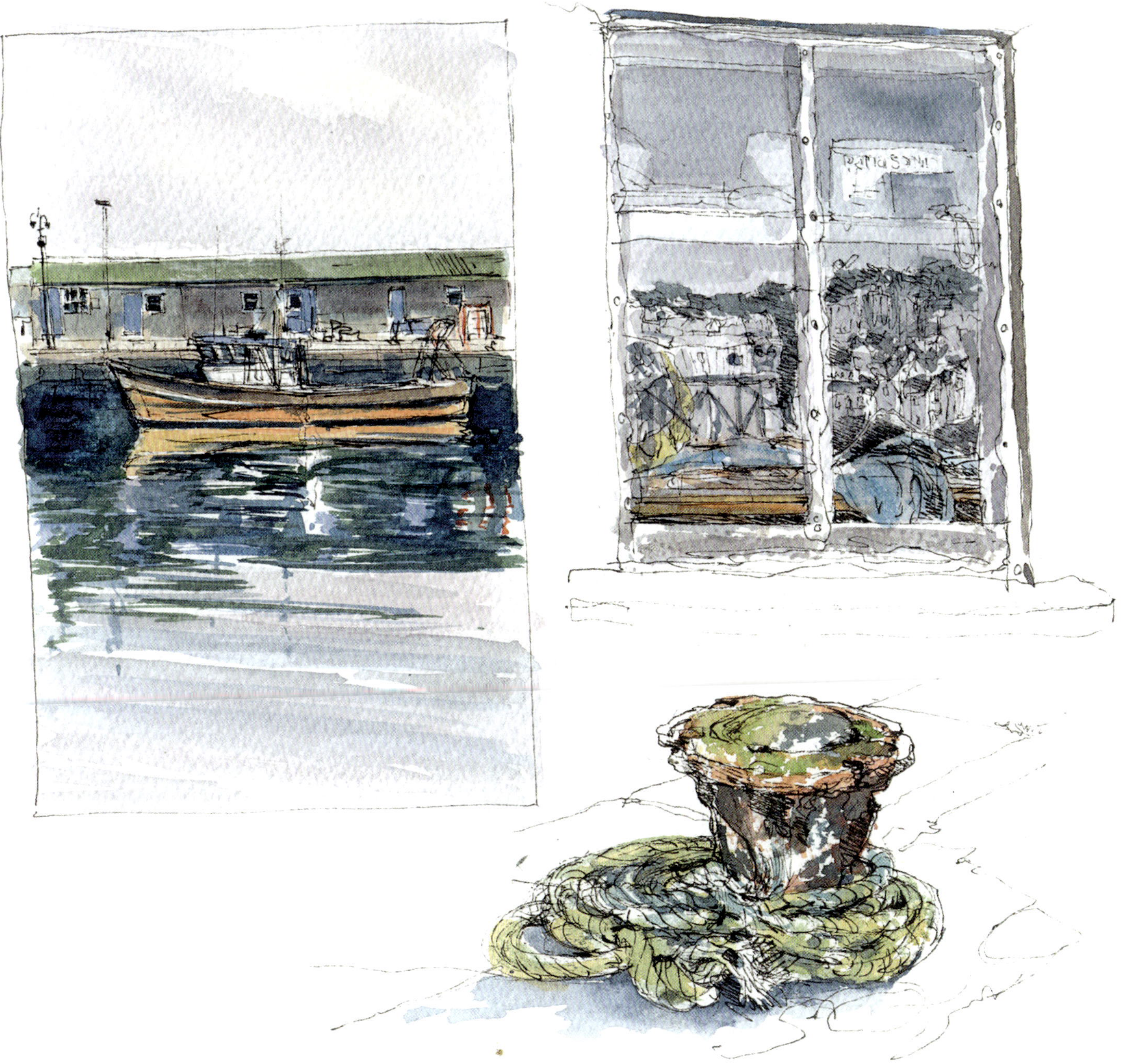

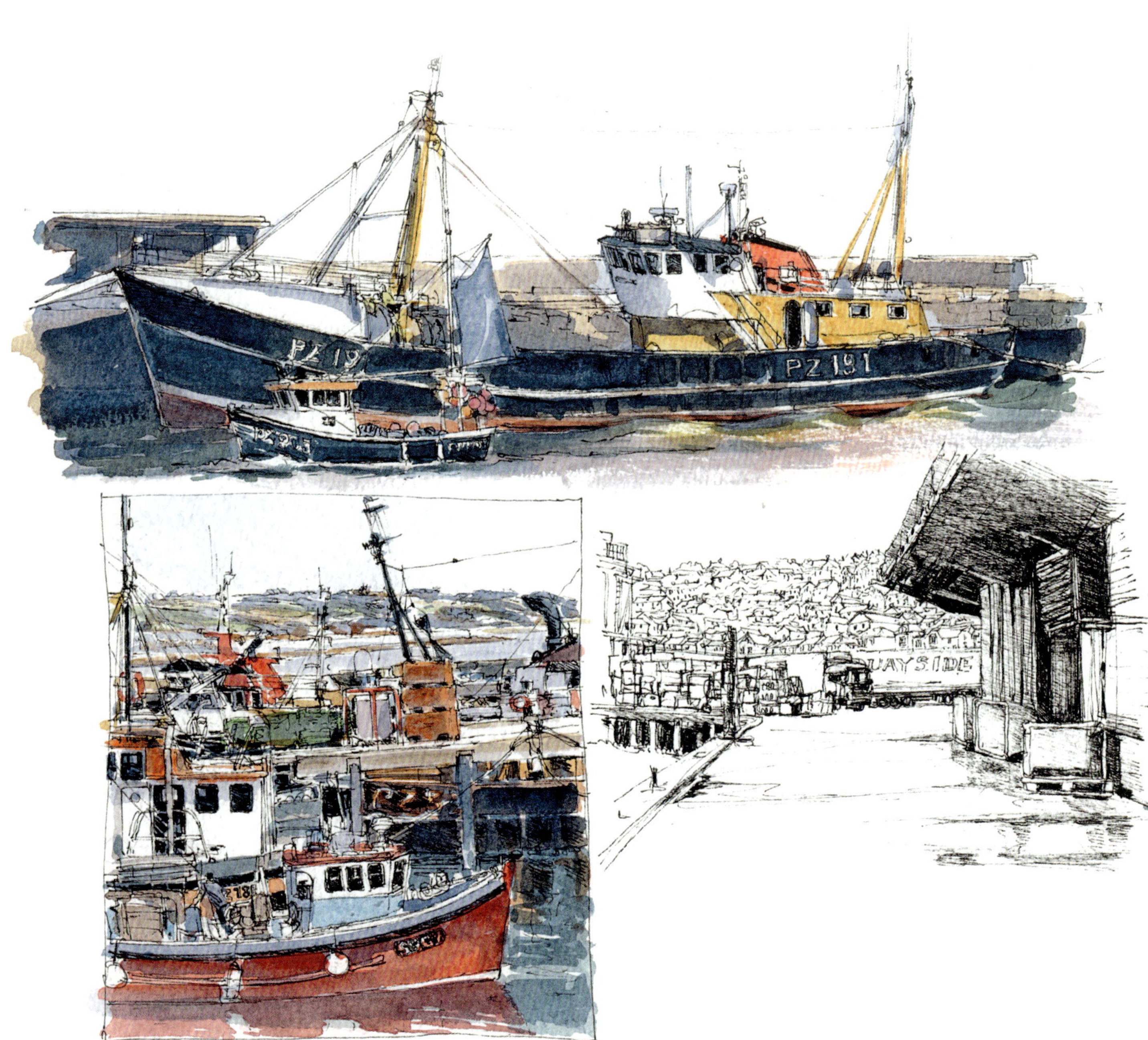
PZ 19
PZ 191
PZ
QUAYSIDE

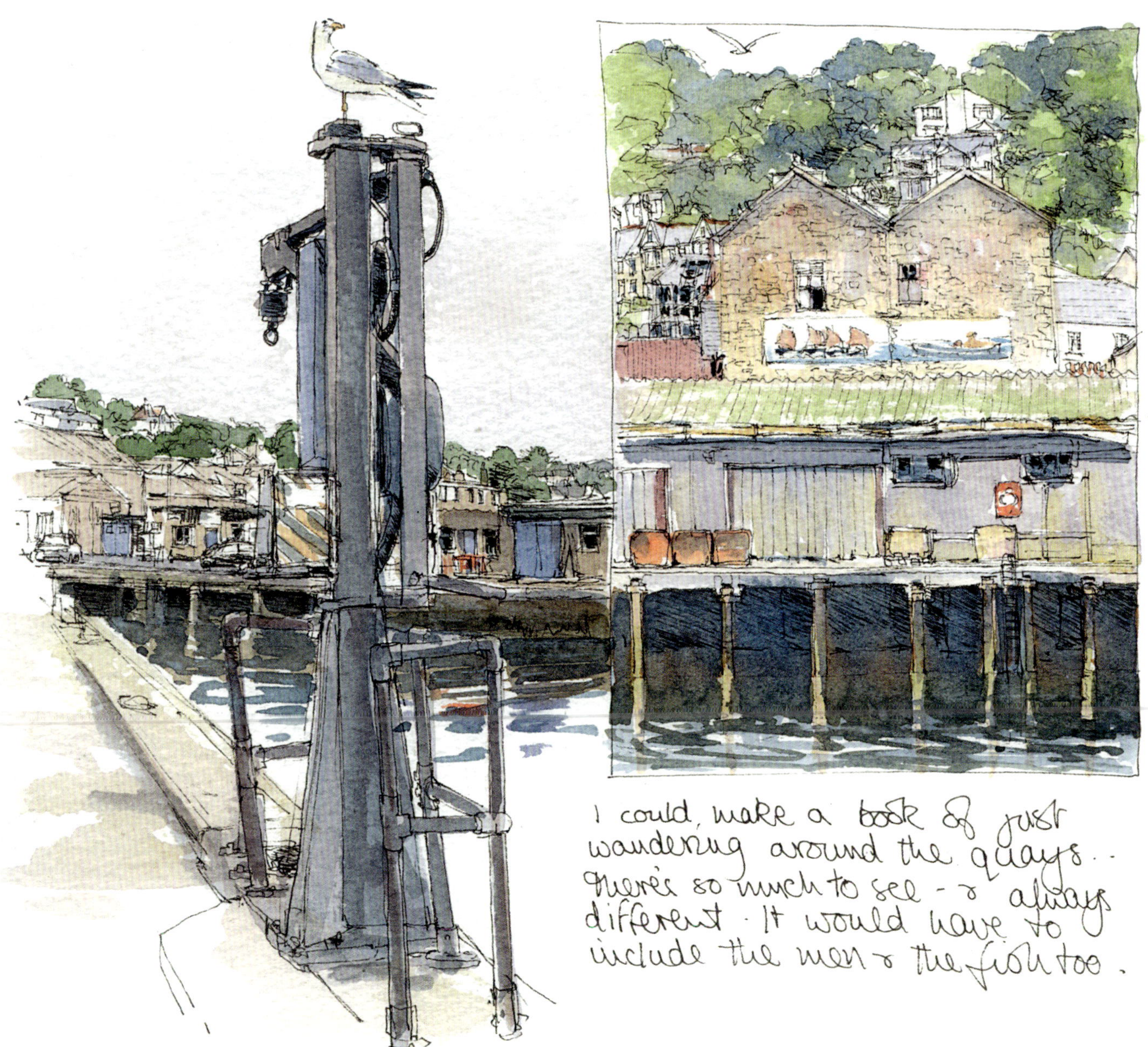

I could make a book of just
wandering around the quays..
there's so much to see - & always
different. It would have to
include the men & the fish too.

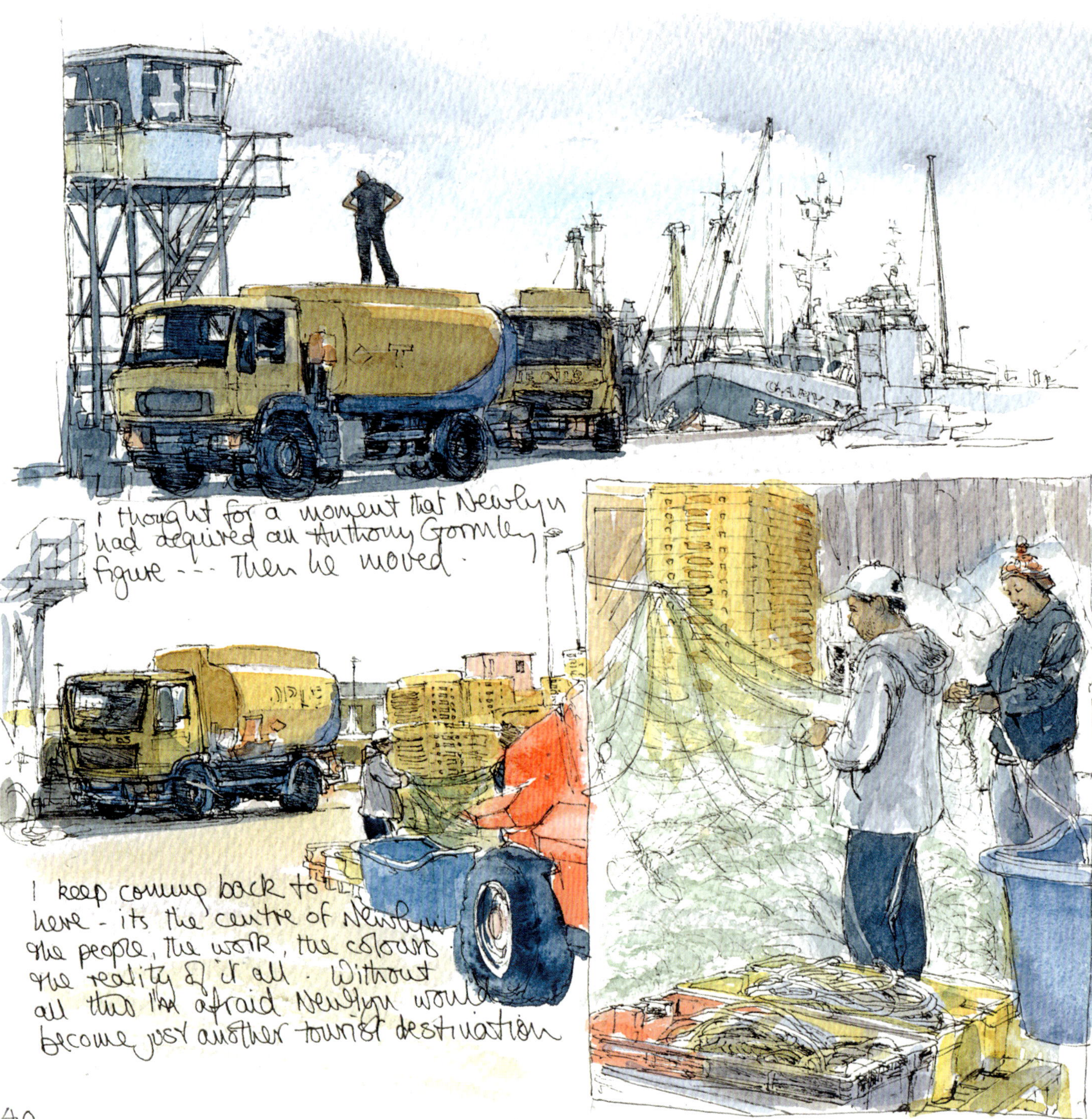

I thought for a moment that Newlyn
had acquired an Anthony Gormley
figure --- Then he moved.

I keep coming back to
here - its the centre of Newlyn
the people, the work, the colours
the reality of it all . Without
all this I'm afraid Newlyn would
become just another tourist destination

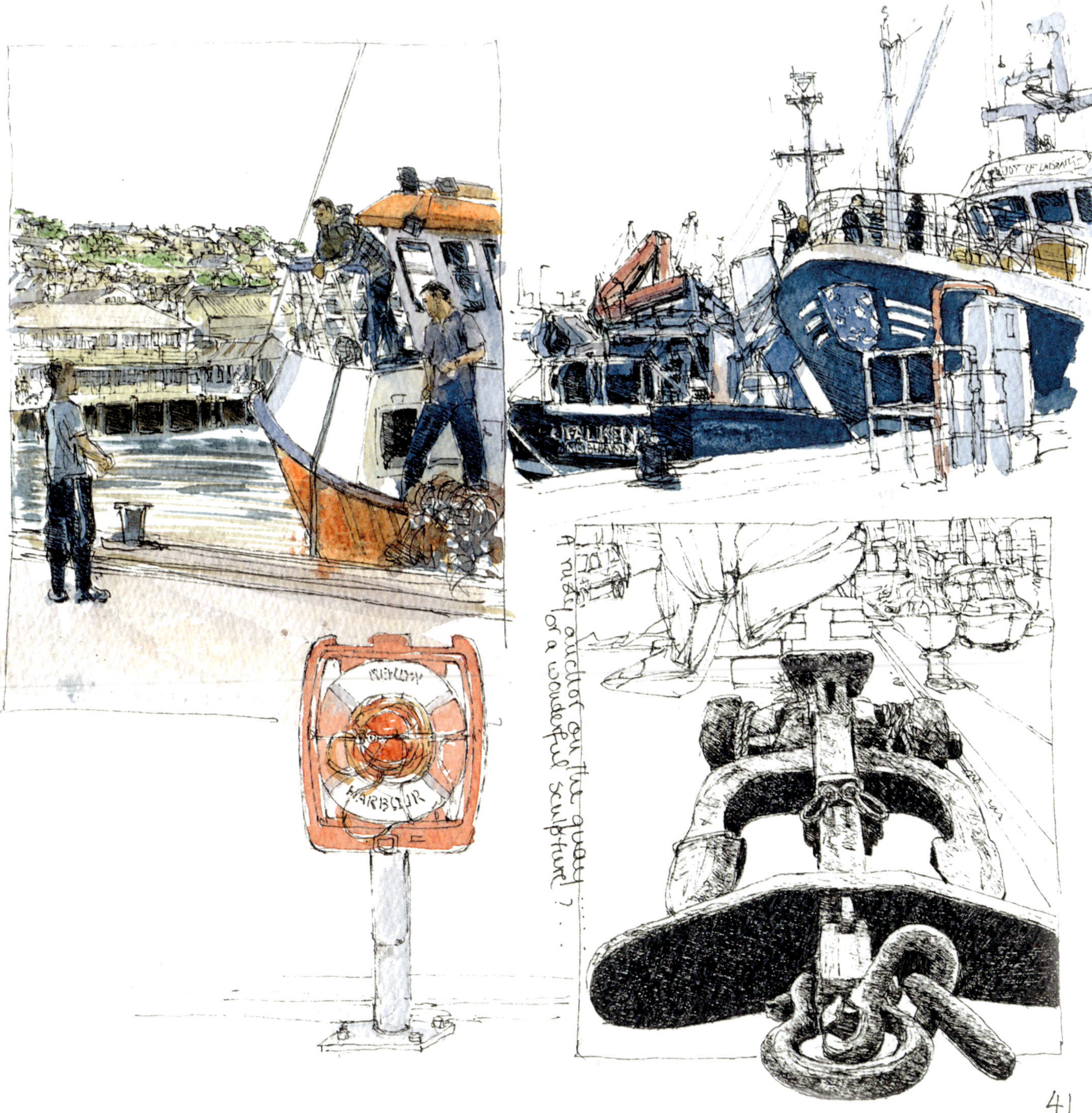

A nice auction on the quay.... or a wonderful sculpture?
HARBOUR
FALKEN
JOY OF LADRAM

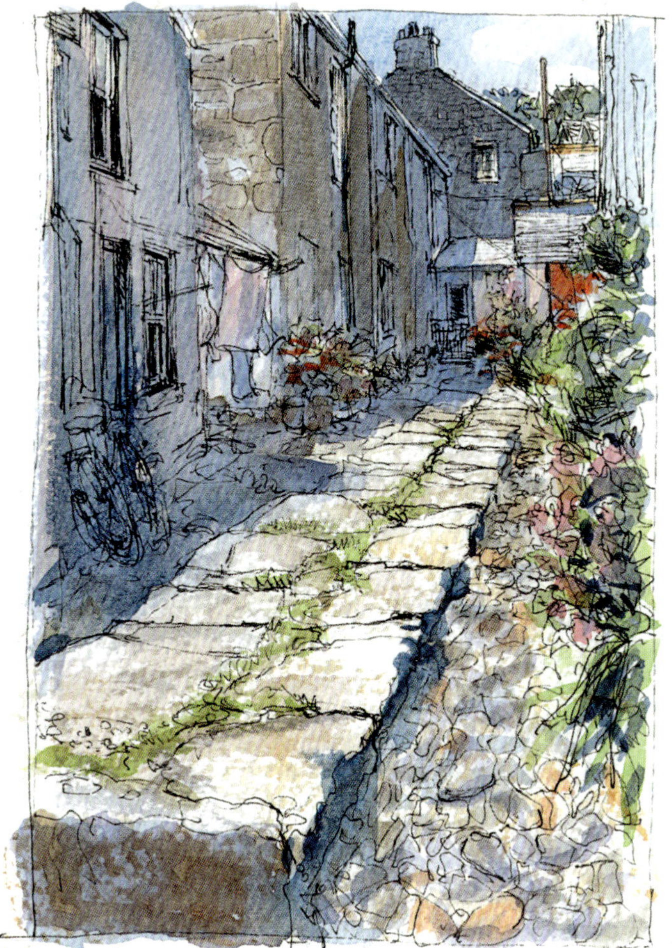

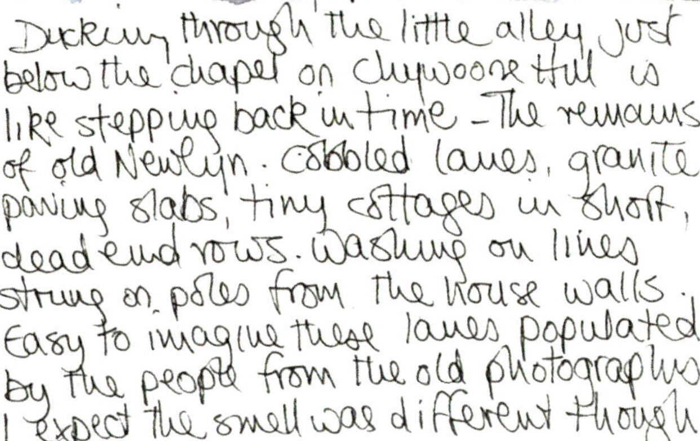

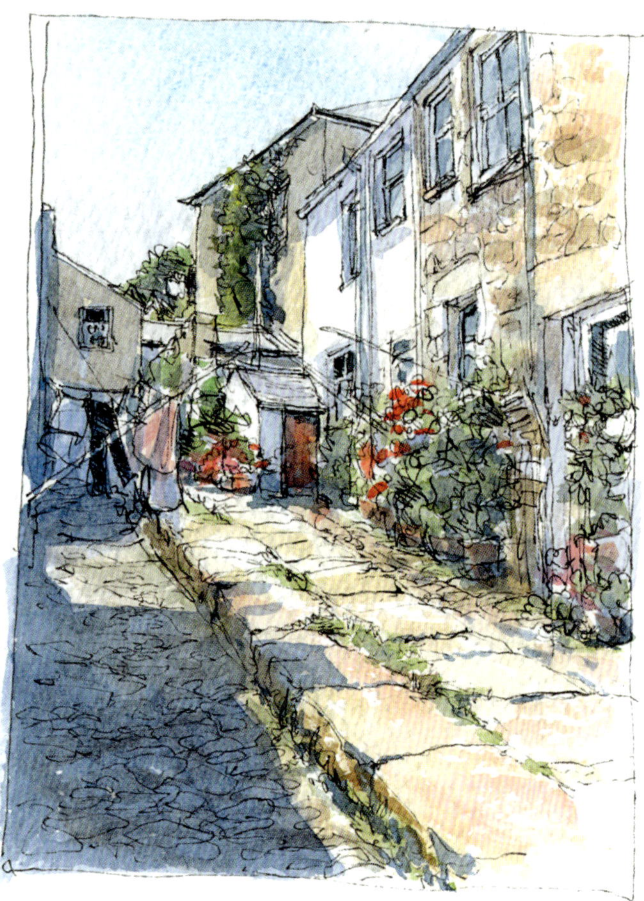

Ducking through the little alley just
below the chapel on Chywoone Hill is
like stepping back in time – The remains
of old Newlyn. Cobbled lanes, granite
paving slabs, tiny cottages in short,
dead end rows. Washing on lines
strung on poles from the house walls.
Easy to imagine these lanes populated
by the people from the old photographs.
I expect the smell was different though.

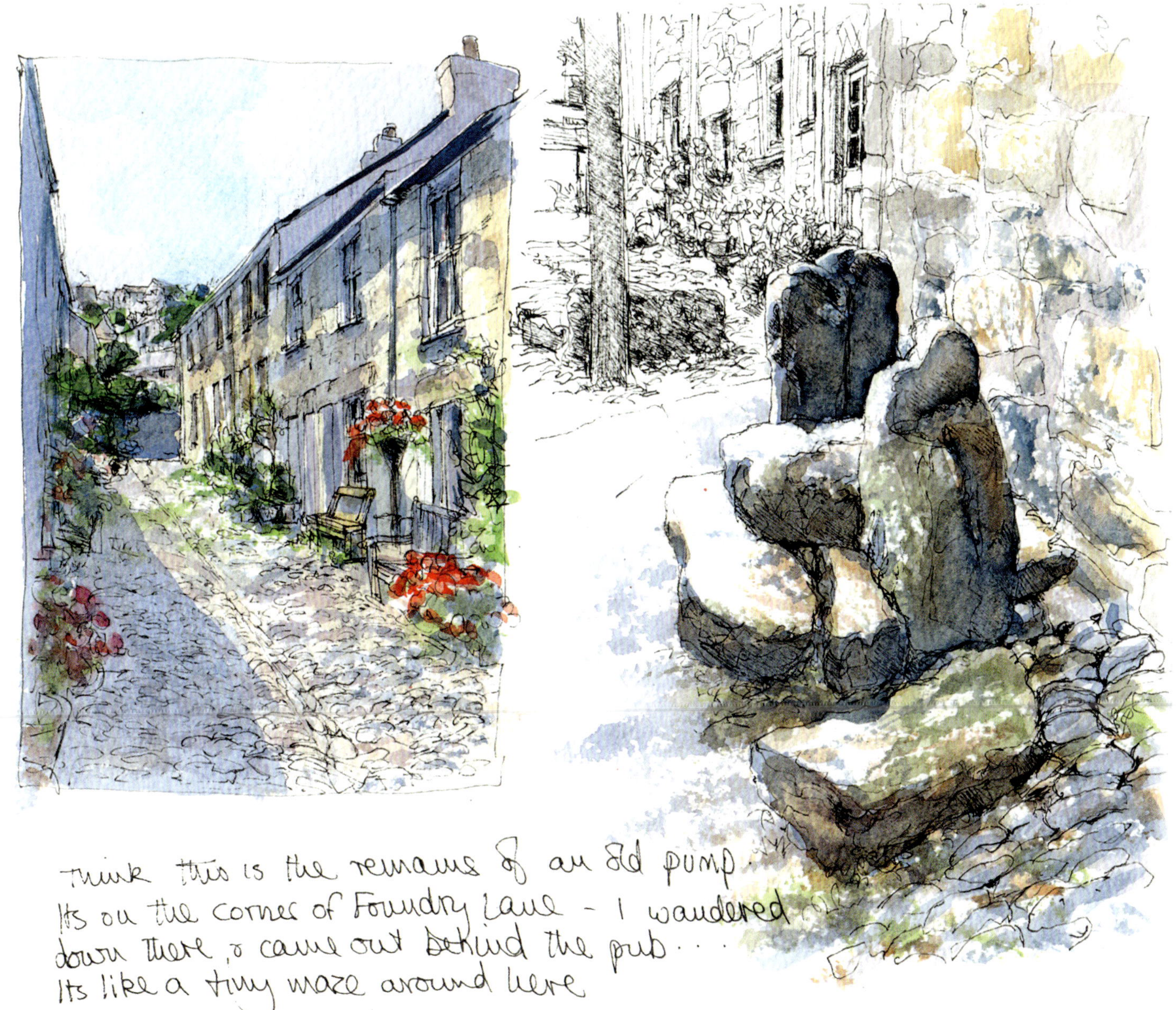

Think this is the remains of an old pump.
Its on the corner of Foundry Lane - I wandered
down there, o came out behind the pub...
Its like a tiny maze around here

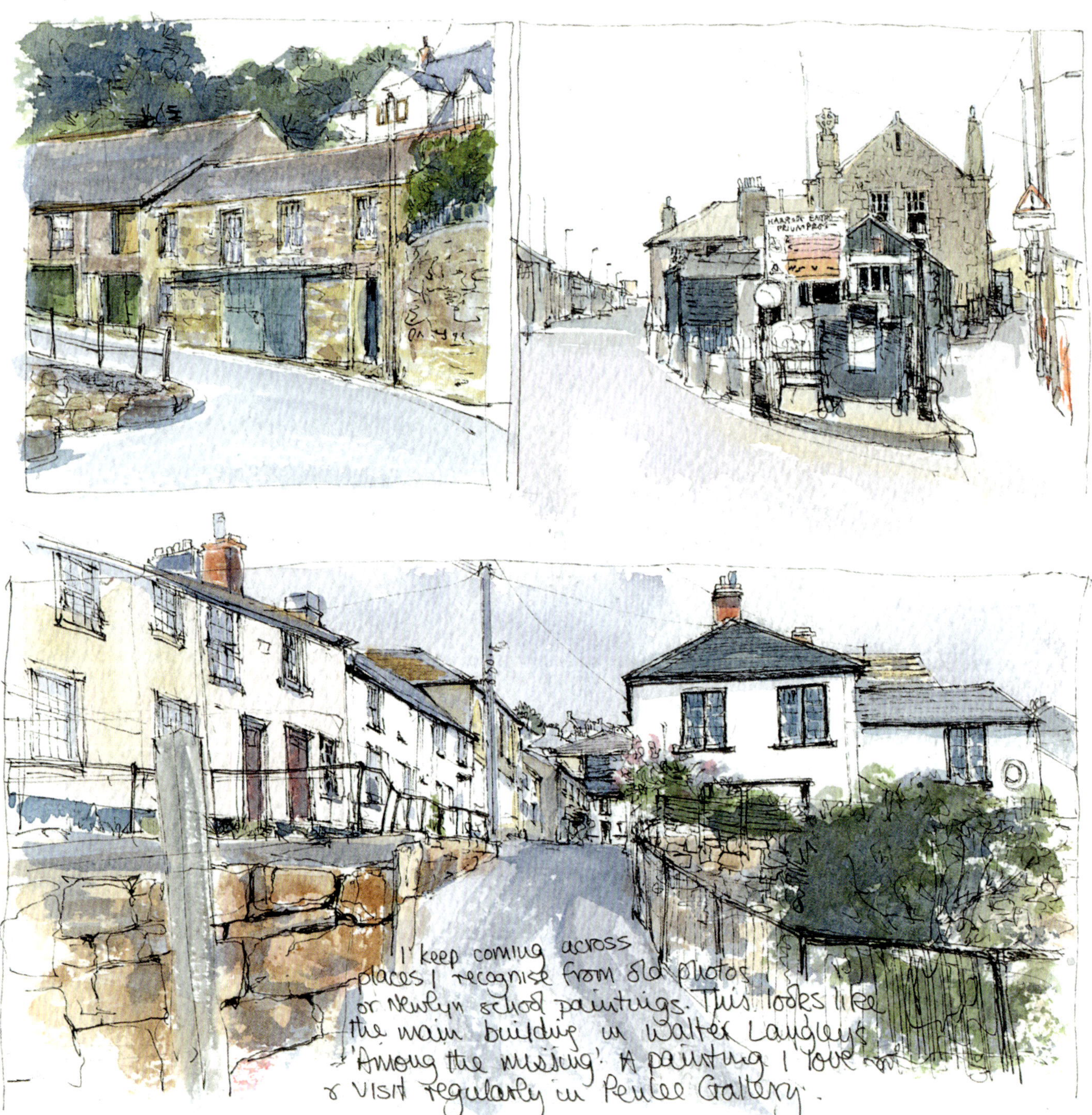

I keep coming across
places I recognise from old photos
or Newlyn school paintings. This looks like
the main building in Walter Langley's
'Among the missing'. A painting I love
& visit regularly in Penlee Gallery.

44

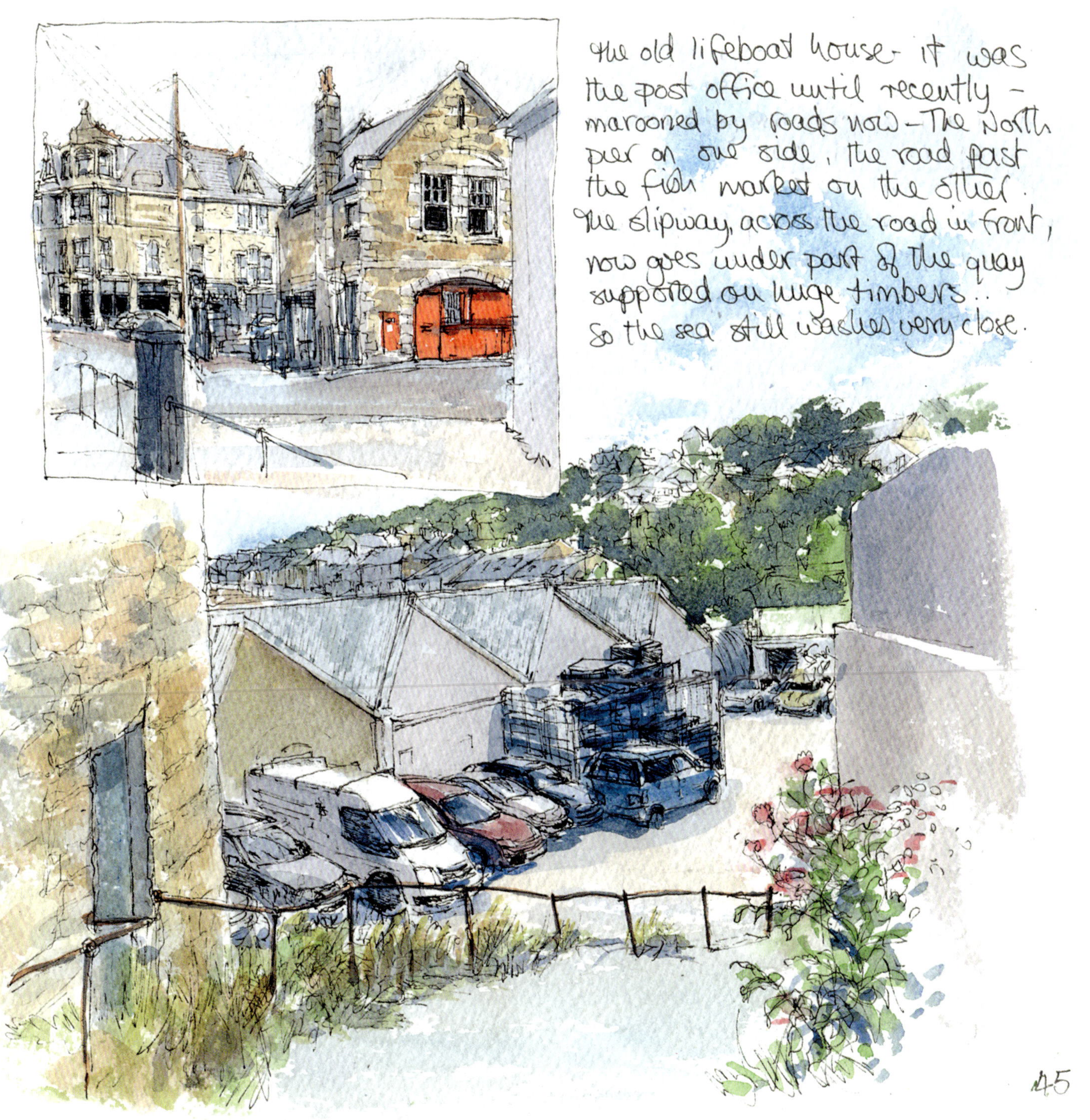

the old lifeboat house - it was
the post office until recently -
marooned by roads now - The North
pier on one side, the road past
the fish market on the other.
The slipway, across the road in front,
now goes under part of the quay
supported on huge timbers ..
So the sea still washes very close.

45

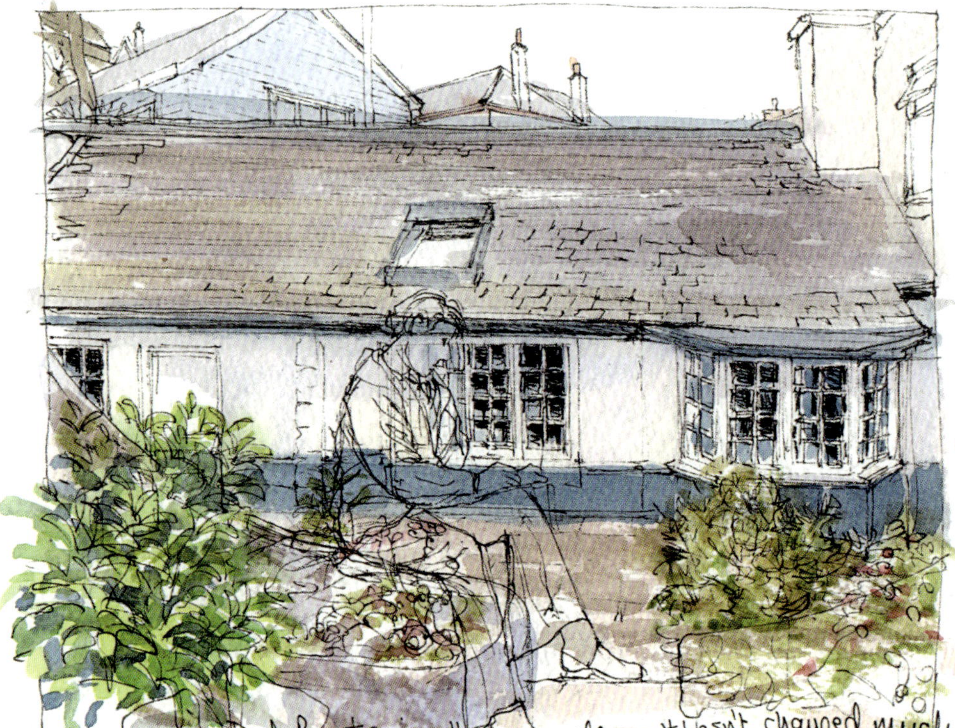

Ernest Procter's studio at North
Corner. In old photos the bay
window is french windows &
the mark of an old wall is
where another open, roofed
building came out at right
angles to another building.
The curved wall - where Dod
sits in a photo is still there.
The studio was a fish cellar?
a pilchard press? A deep
cobbled drain runs outside
the wall to the house. The
front & back doors were
lined up so fish etc
could be carried through
easily.

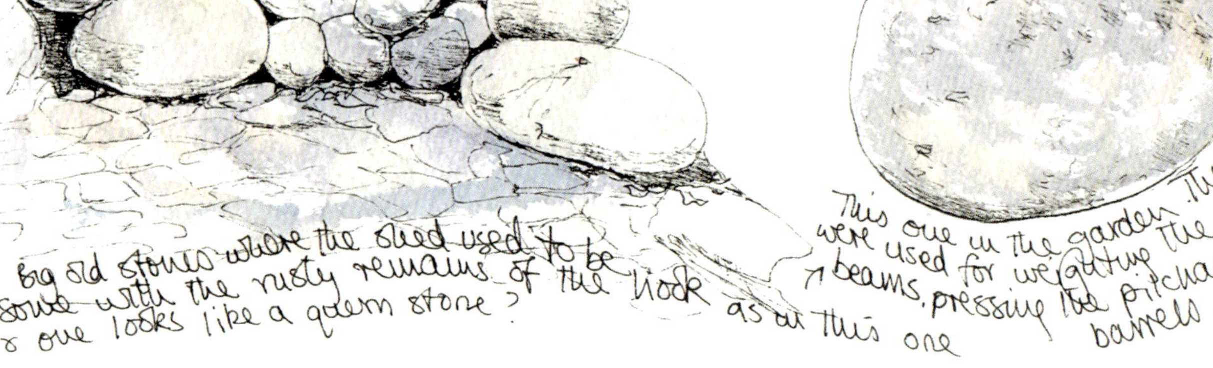

Dod Procter in the garden - It hasn't changed much.

The garden is still very beautiful...

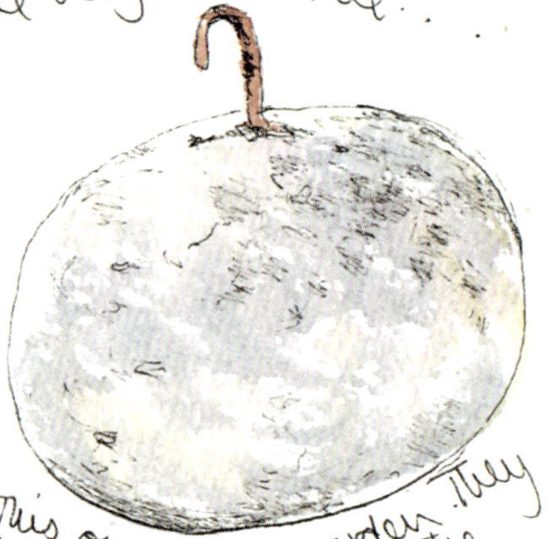

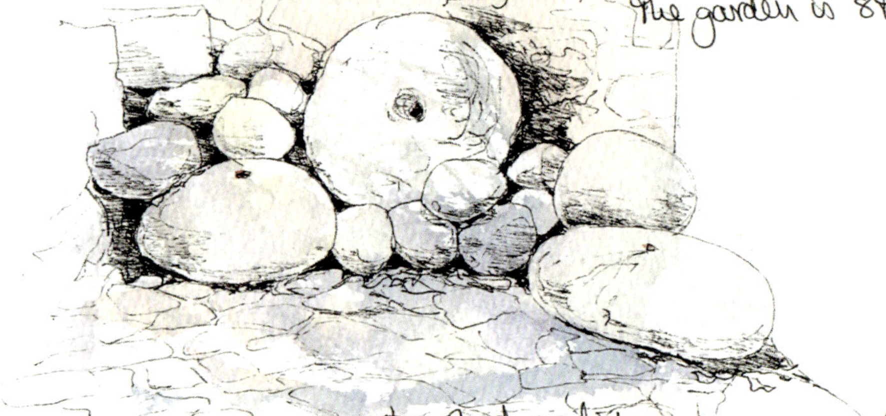

Big old stones where the shed used to be
some with the rusty remains of the hook as in this one
& one looks like a quern stone?

This one in the garden. They
were used for weighting the
beams, pressing the pilchard
barrels.

46

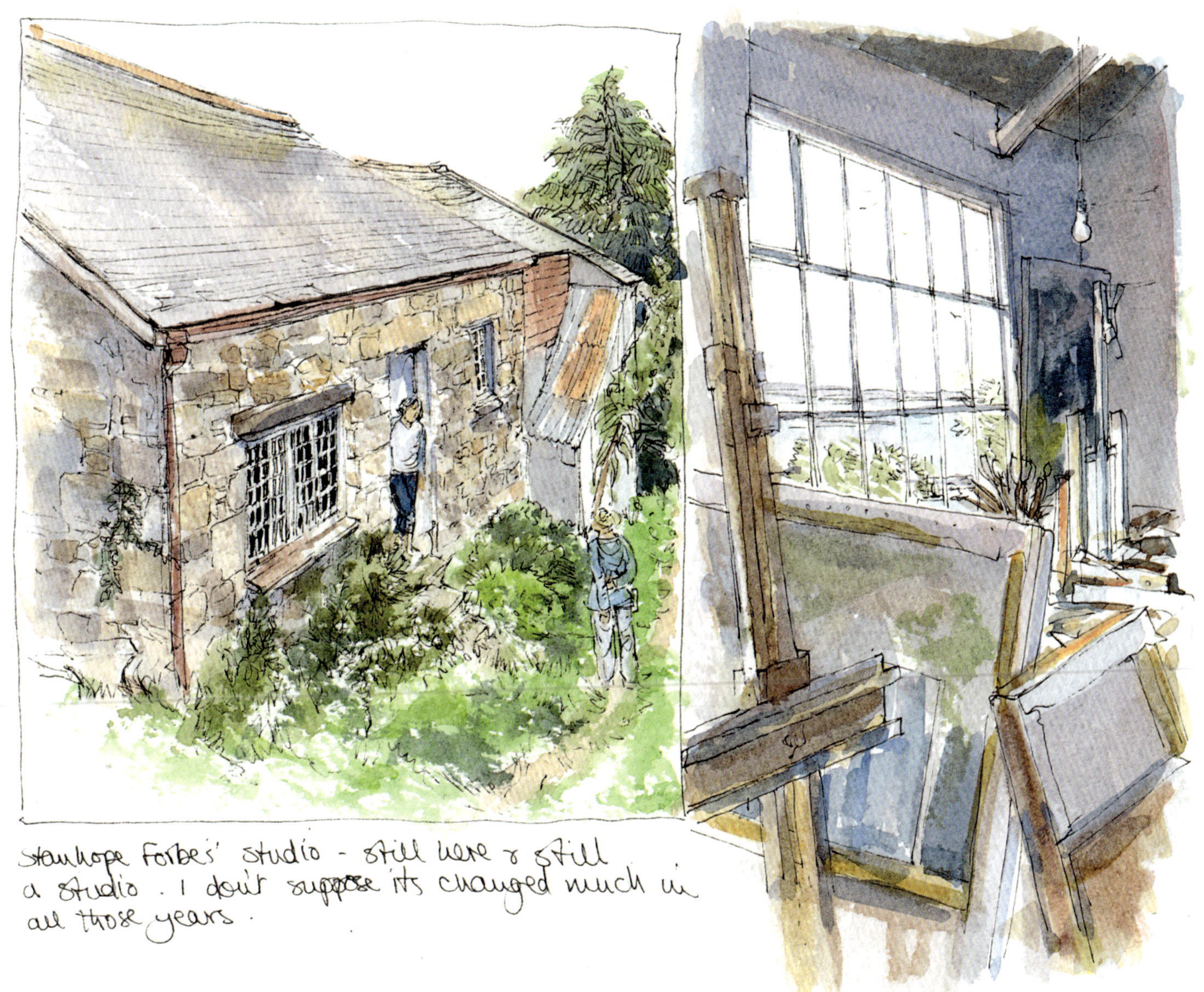

Stanhope Forbes' studio - still here & still
a studio. I don't suppose it's changed much in
all those years.

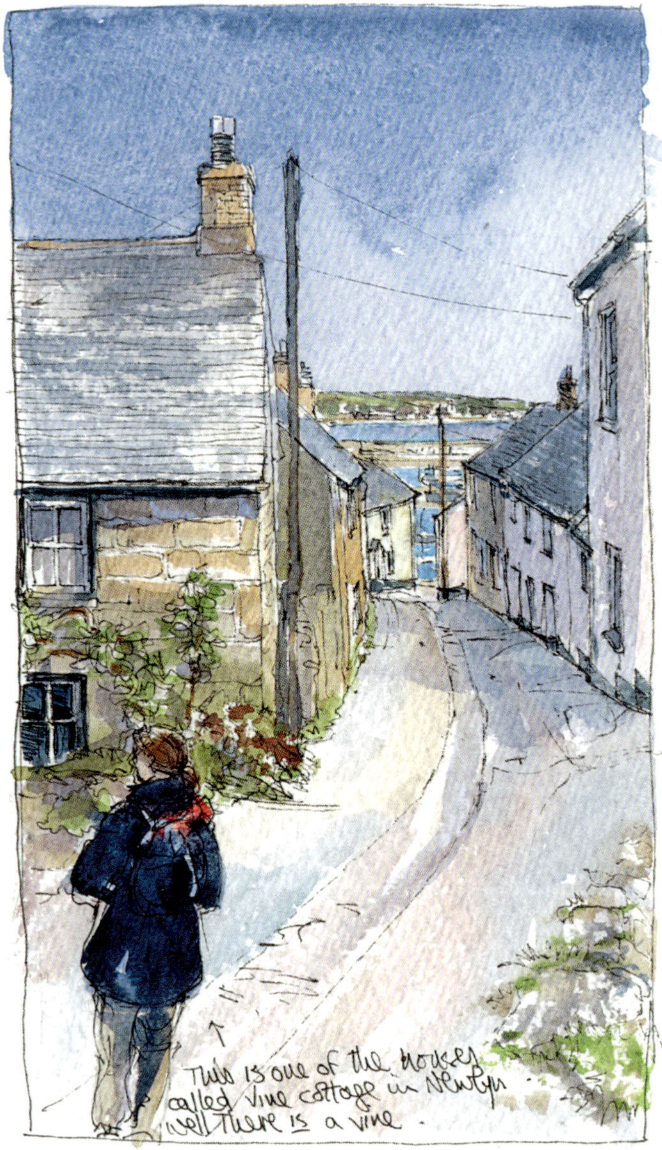

This is one of the houses
called Vine cottage in Newlyn
well there is a vine.

I keep wandering through tiny alleys,
gaps between houses winding through
little 'courts', tiny gardens... & I keep
coming across 'High Mountains'...
But only when I'm not looking for it.

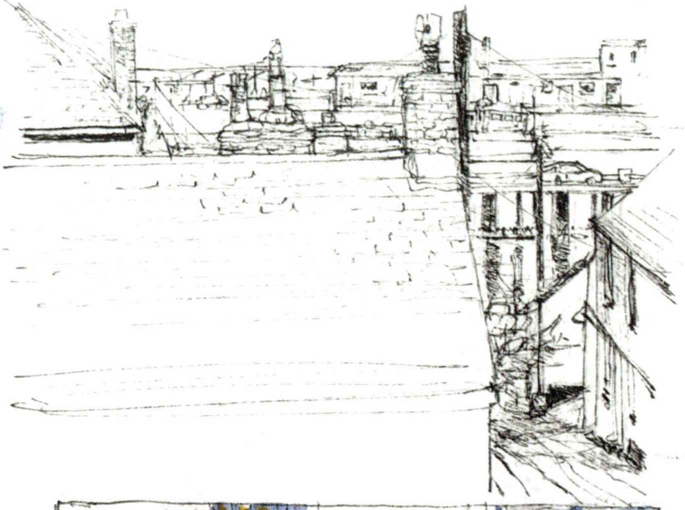

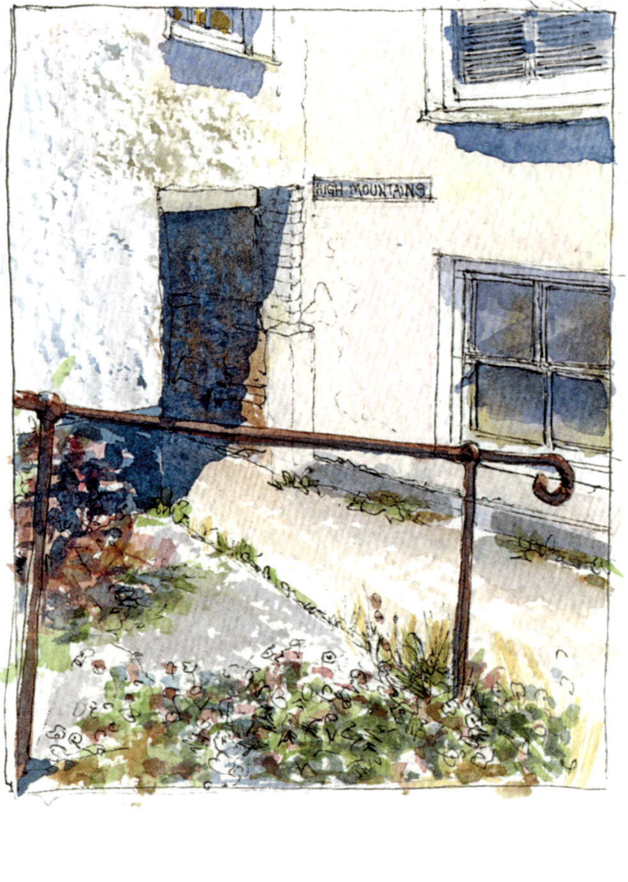

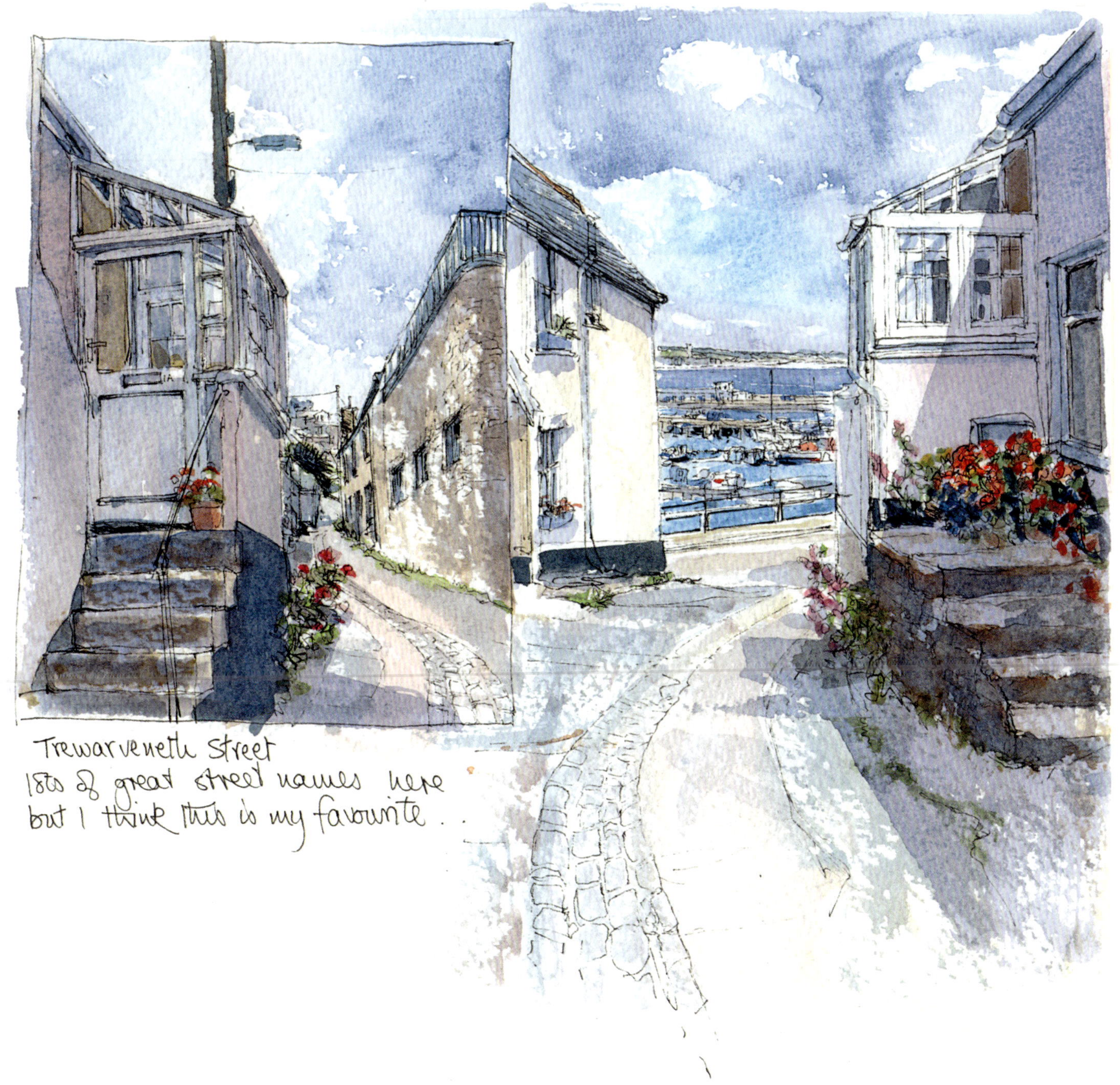

Trewarveneth street
lots of great street names here
but I think this is my favourite . .

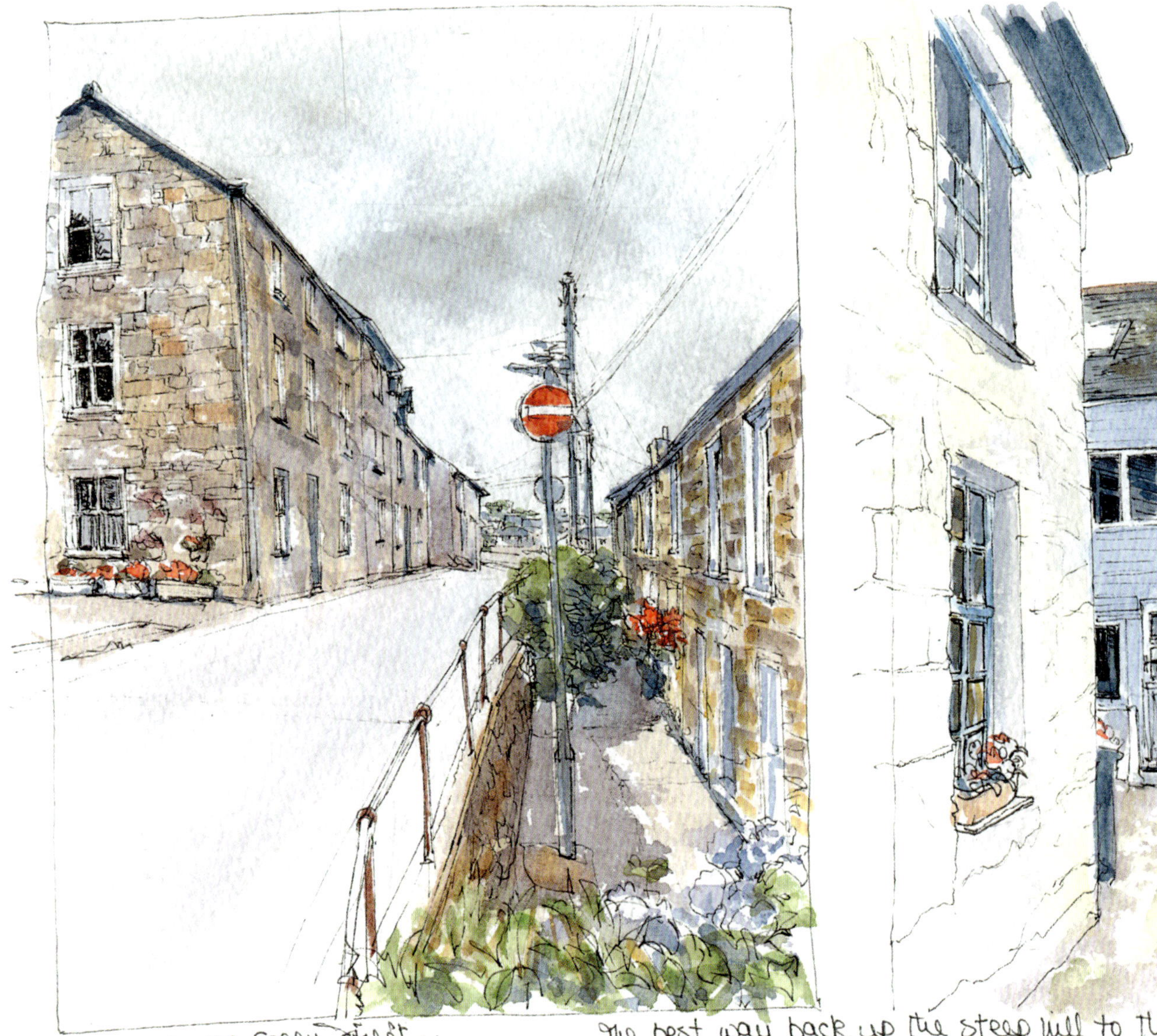

Upper & Lower Green Street..
Now - the Narrows.

The best way back up the steep hill to the car
parked at Steph's is this - wander up to Mary's for
a coffee & a chat, slowly up 'Breakneck alley' Stop
to admire the view up St Peter's Hill. Then round
by Myrtle cottage & on up Gwavas Road. Admire
the view down Bowjey Hill & I'm there..

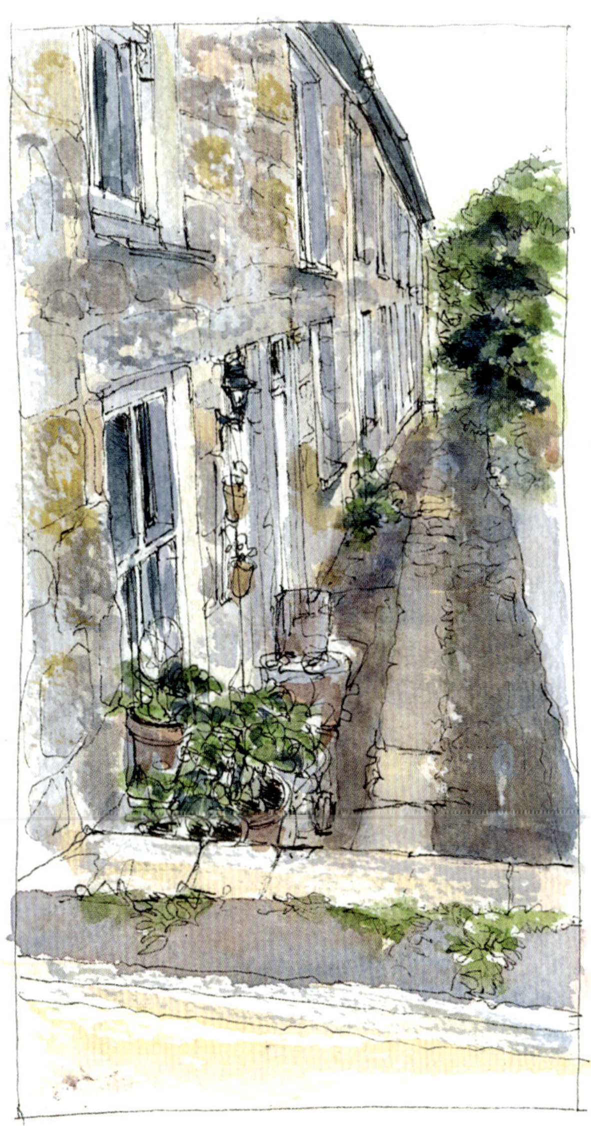

Ebenezer Terrace

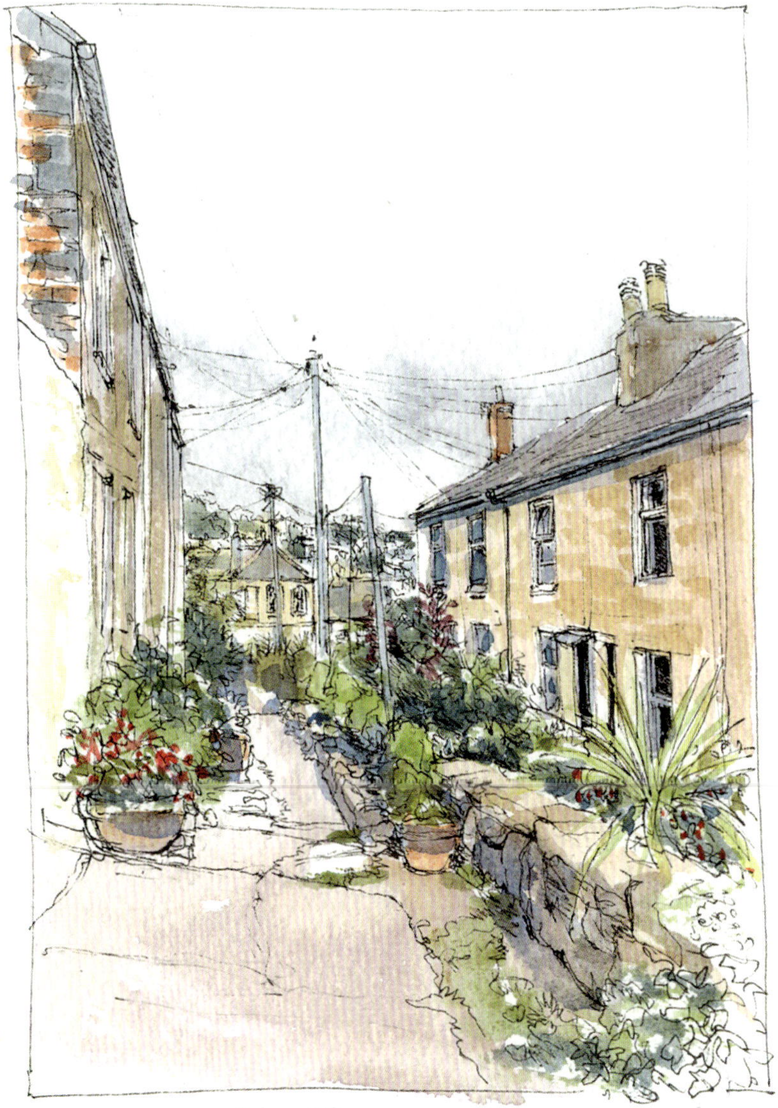

Eden Terrace

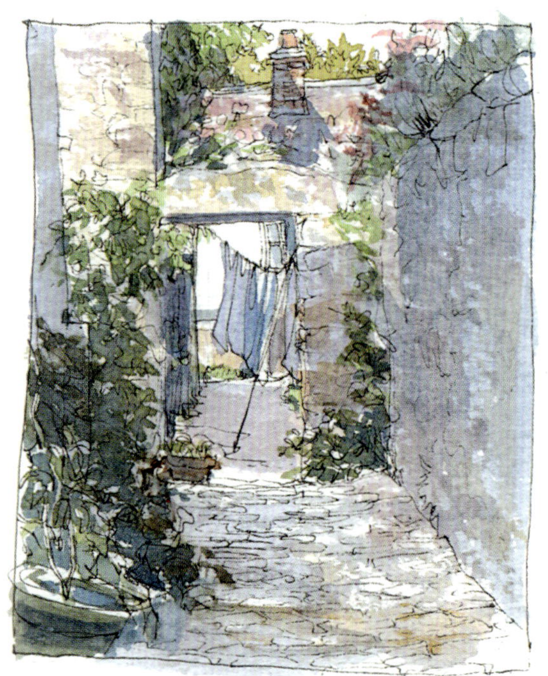

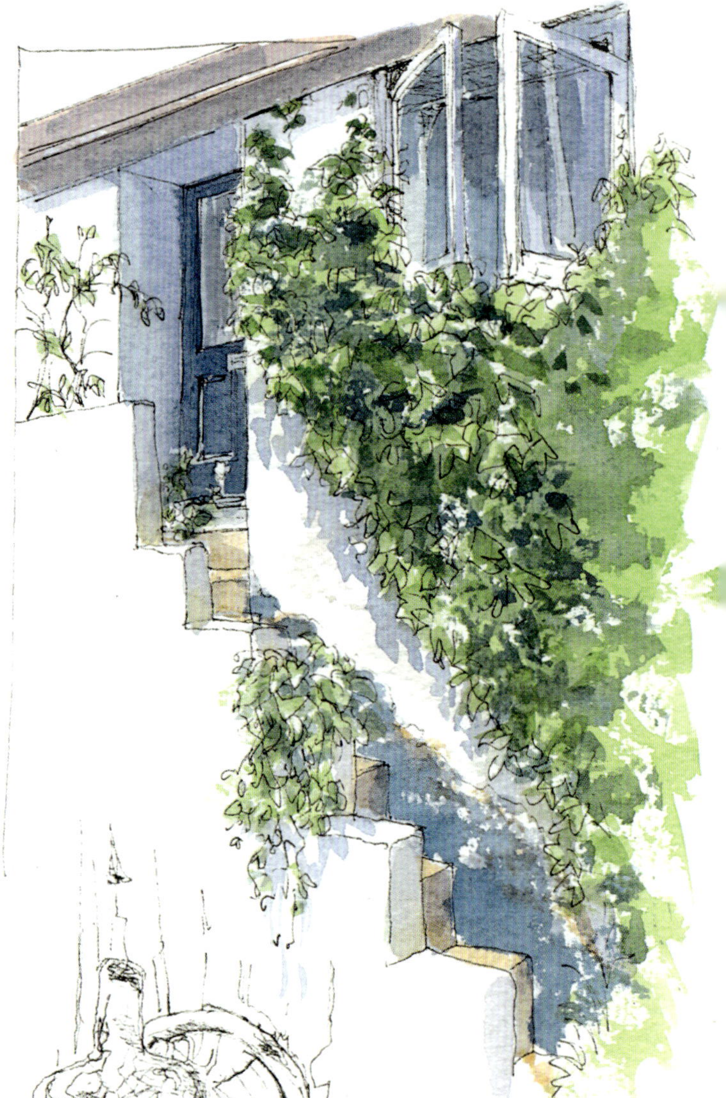

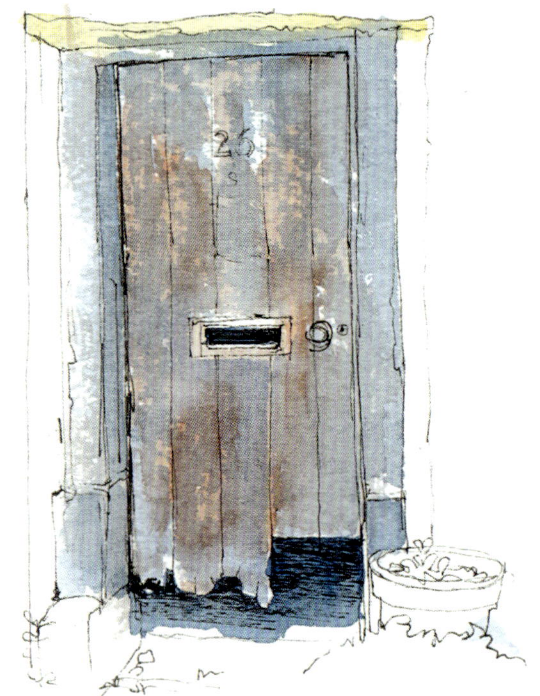

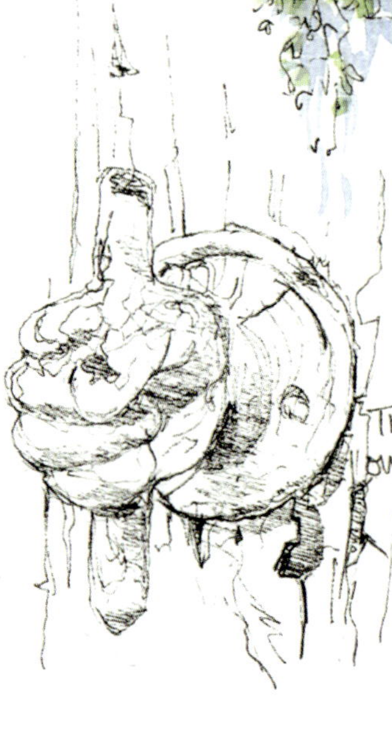

This is the door handle on what might be a garden door? Thanks Steph for spotting it . .

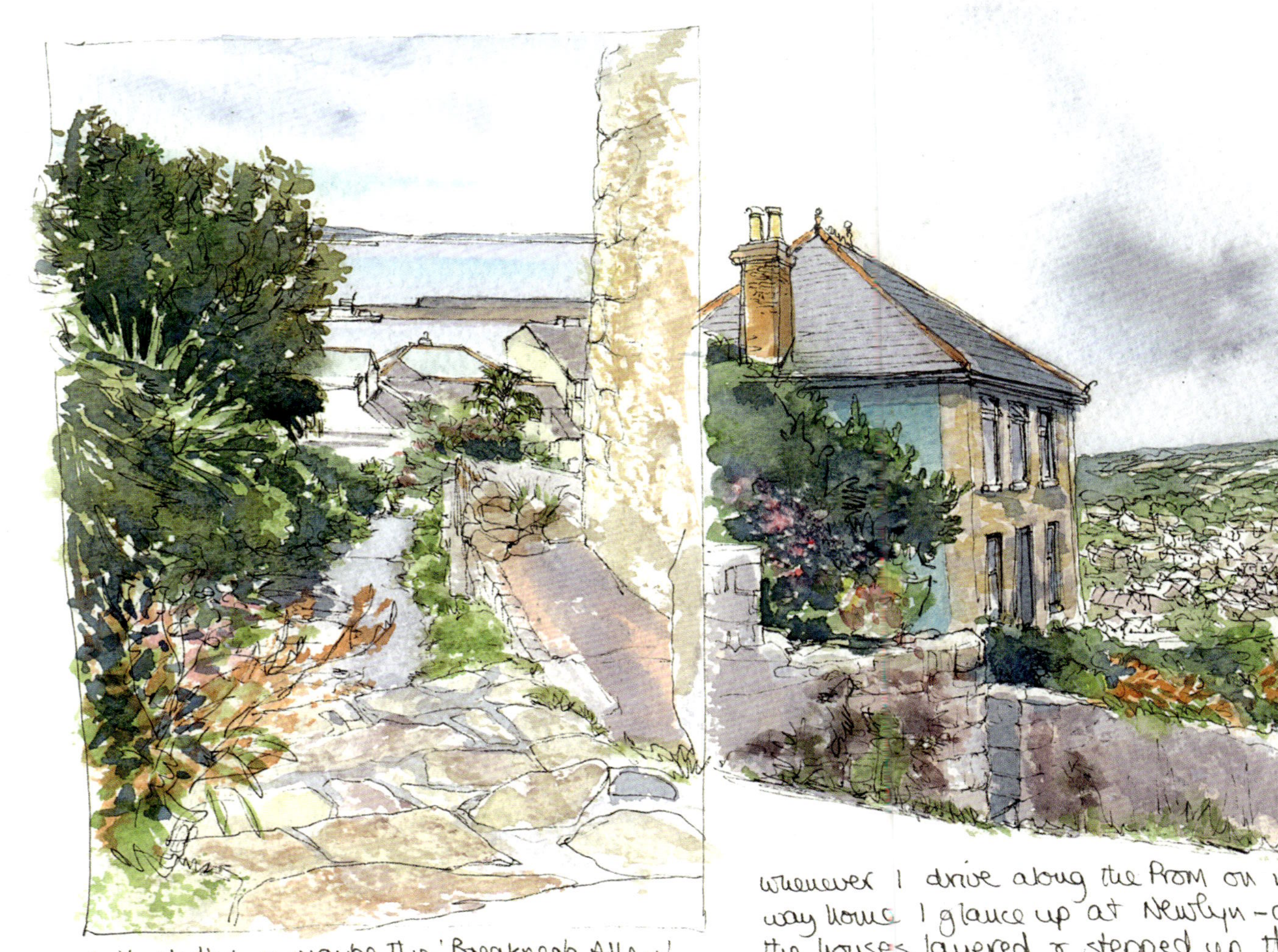

I think this is maybe the 'Breakneck Alley'
talked about as going steeply down into
Duke St & Primrose Court – long gone in the
1980's "slum clearance" & now a car park..
It has steps now in places. Could it be
the one?

Whenever I drive along the Prom on my
way home I glance up at Newlyn – all
the houses layered & stepped up the
hill above the harbour. One tall thin house
jumps out – painted a deep blue/turquoise.
I couldn't find it when walking up & down
the lanes – until, toiling up towards Gwavas
I turned to breath deeply (& look at the view)
& there it is. I've obviously not looked
back from this point before.

Swans in the distance - lovely
Swans up close - not so good...
I'm scared of geese too!

...have walked down this slipway lots
of times & never seen it's beautiful
patterns - & walked straight past this
overgrown anchor too

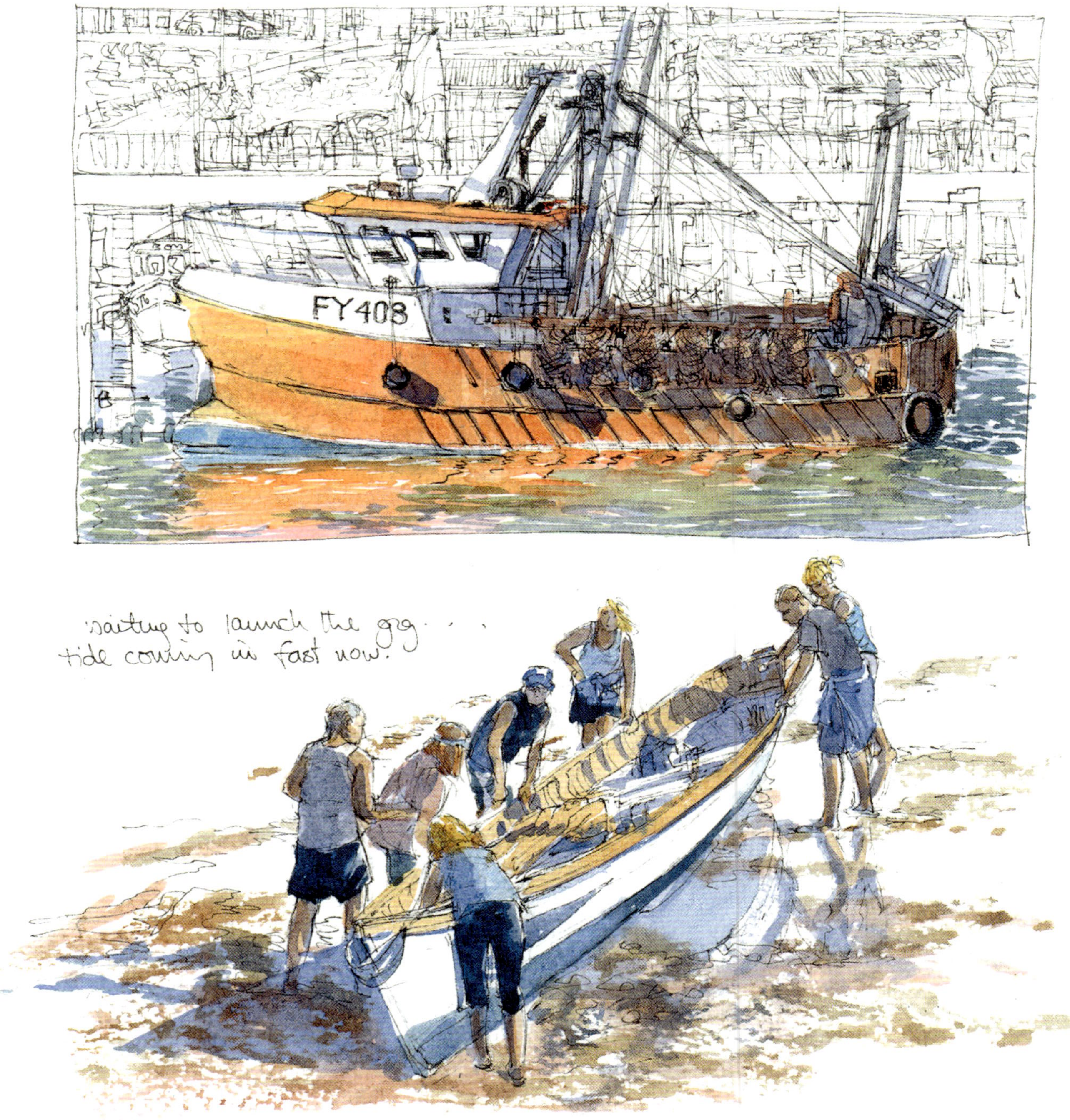

waiting to launch the gig . . .
tide coming in fast now.

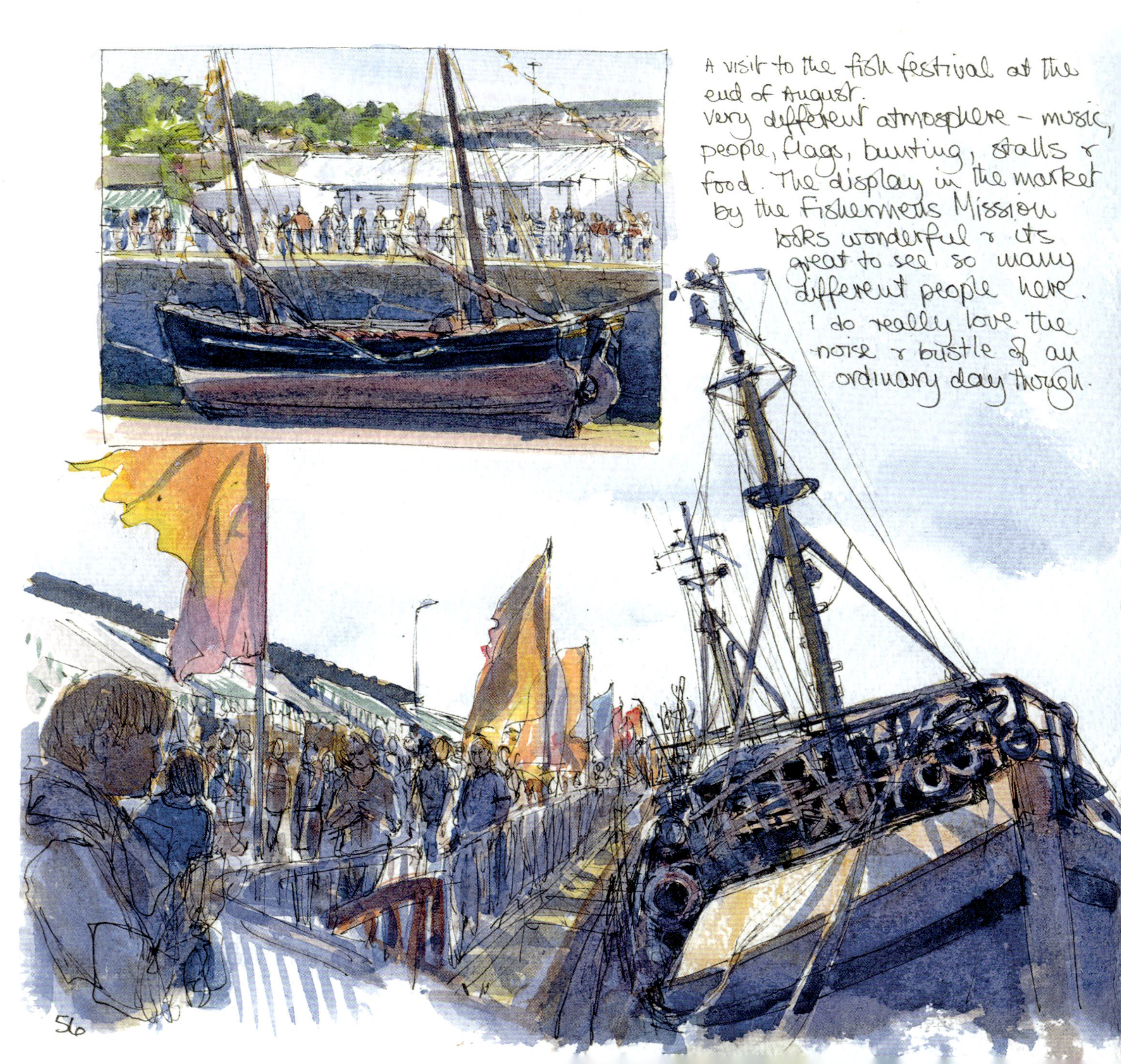
A visit to the fish festival at the
end of August.
Very different atmosphere — music,
people, flags, bunting, stalls &
food. The display in the market
by the Fishermens Mission
looks wonderful & its
great to see so many
different people here.
I do really love the
noise & bustle of an
ordinary day though.
56

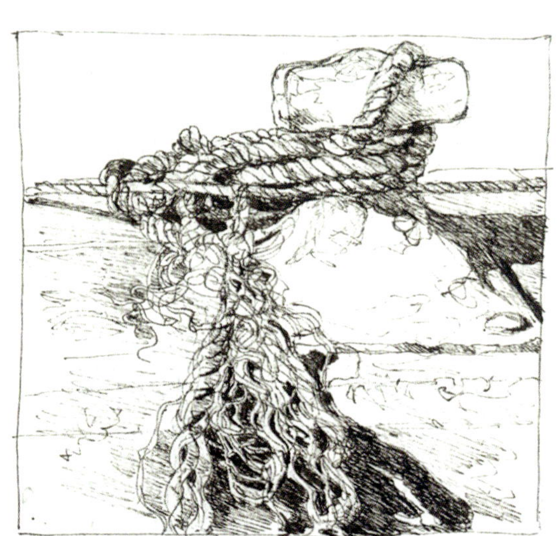

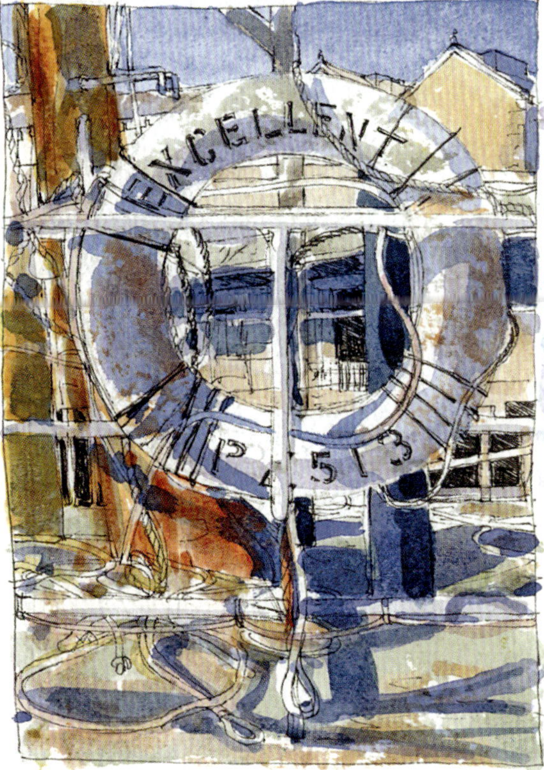
EXCELLENT
PZ 513

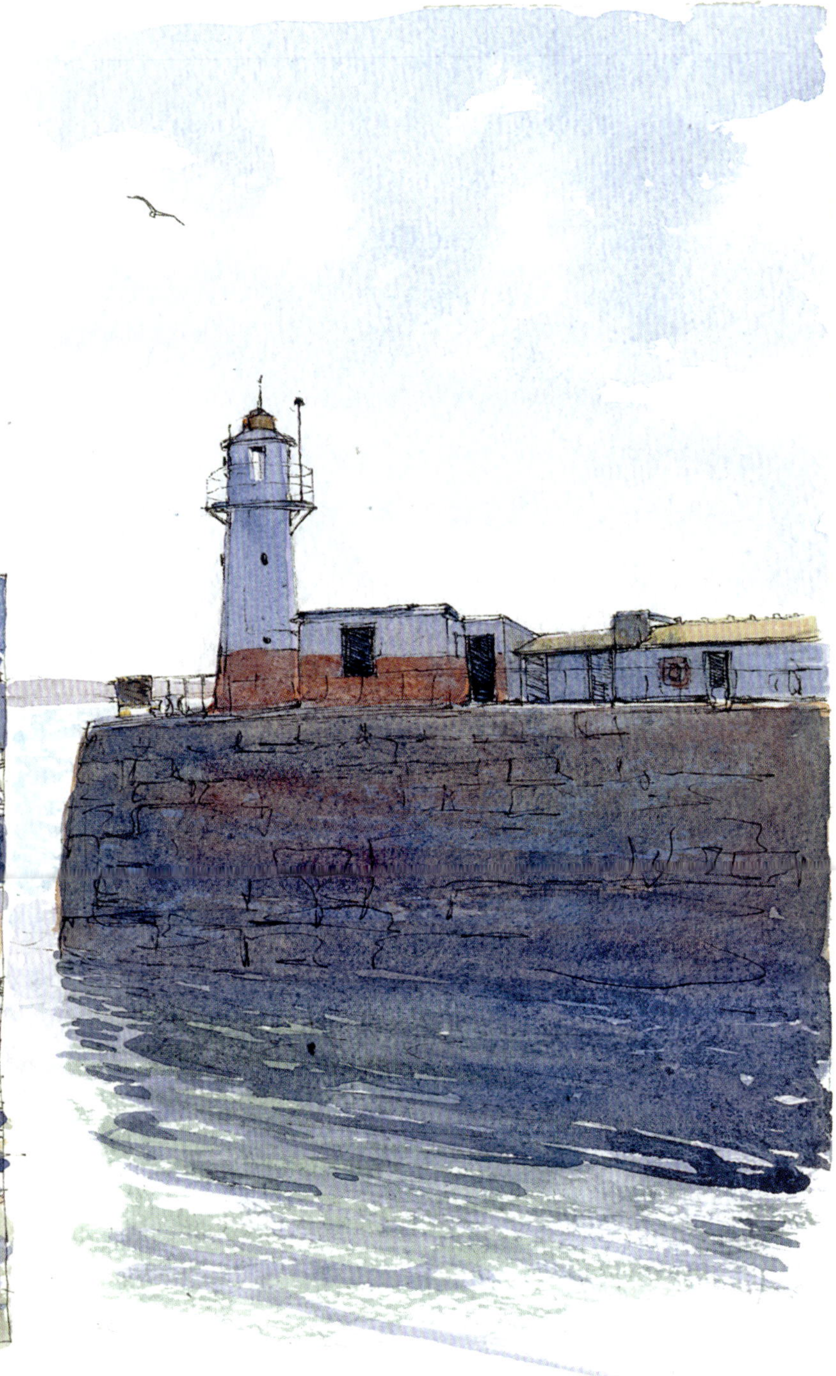

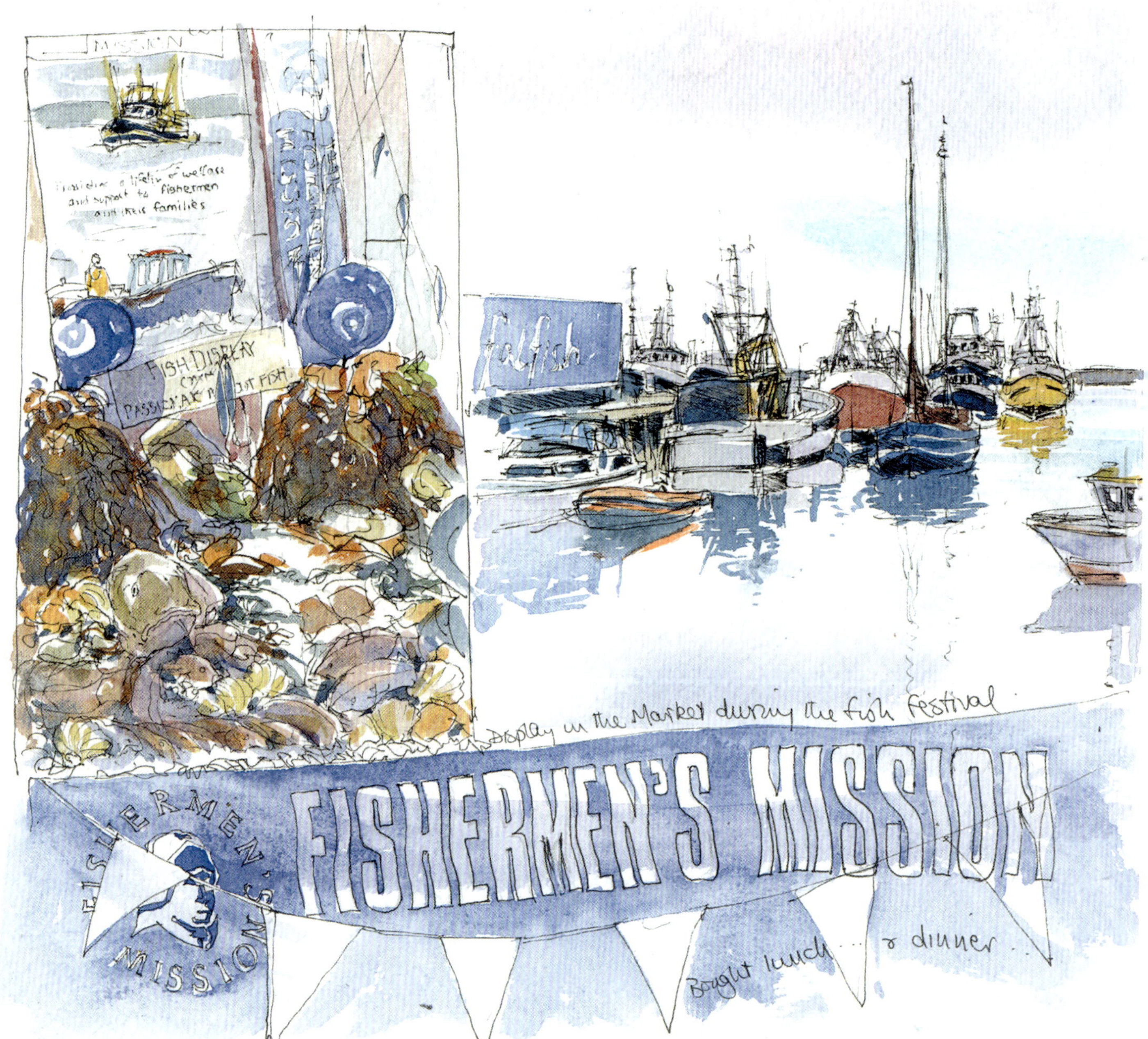

MISSION
Providing a lifetime of welfare and support to fishermen and their families
FISH DISPLAY
PASSIONATE ABOUT FISH
falfish
Display in the Market during the fish Festival
FISHERMEN'S MISSION
FISHERMEN'S MISSIONS
Bought lunch ... r dinner

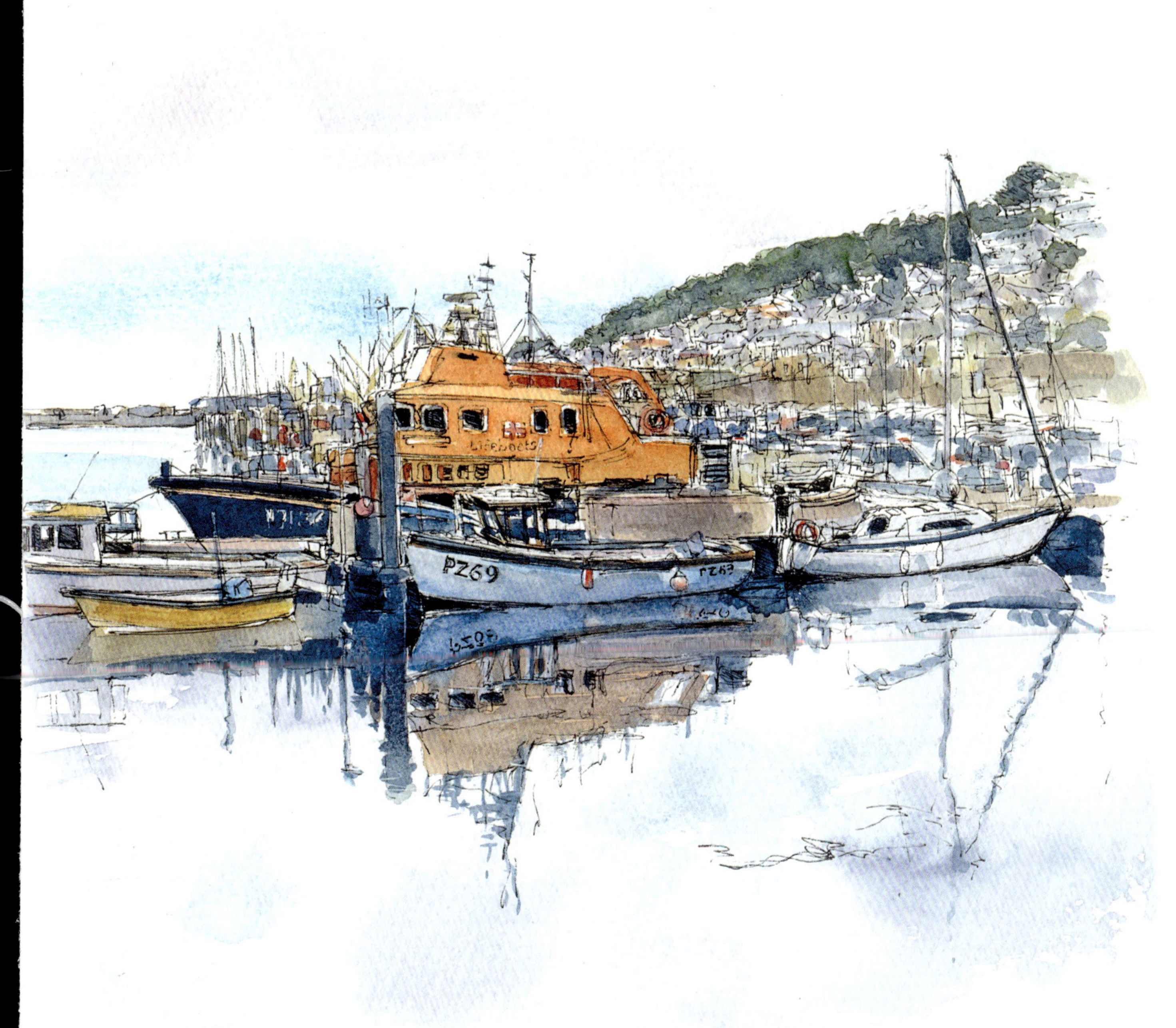
Lifeboats
PZ69

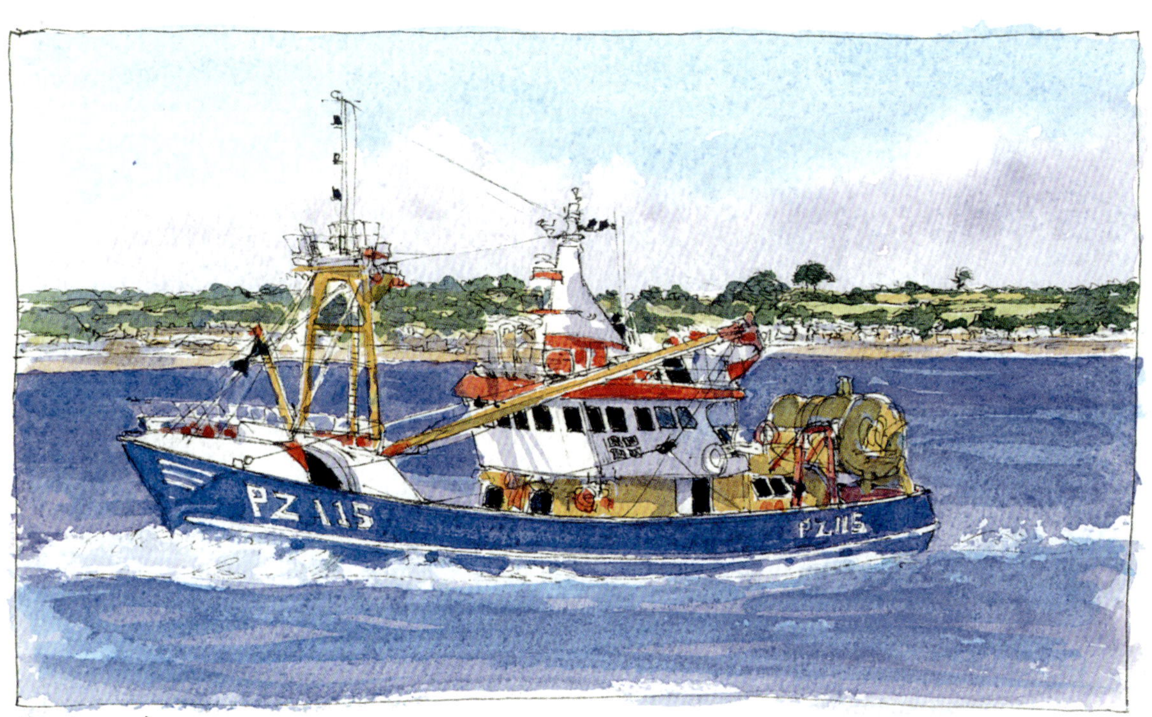

Heading home